HIGH SOBRIETY

A trip out of the bottle into your intuition

Rae Leonard

Platypus Publishing

For more information contact: rae@raeleonard.me

Book Cover Design: Abby Sierros
Project Manager: Karina Antonopoulos

Printed in the United States of America

ISBN: 978-1-959555-82-7

This book is for you, my dearest reader.

If something here helps you make a more intuitive, a more informed choice about your life and your happiness, I am grateful.

TABLE OF CONTENTS

TIME IS A MANMADE CONSTRUCT
FREQUENCY IS EVERYTHING
DAYS OF GRATITUDE
NIGHTLIFE
FALL FLAT ON YOUR FAITH

"Nothing is original. Steal from anywhere that resonates with inspiration or fuels your imagination. Devour old films, new films, music, books, paintings, photographs, poems, dreams, random conversations, architecture, bridges, street signs, trees, clouds, bodies of water, light and shadows. Select only things to steal from that speak directly to your soul. If you do this, your work (and theft) will be authentic. Authenticity is invaluable; originality is non-existent. And don't bother concealing your thievery - celebrate it if you feel like it. In any case, always remember what Jean-Luc Godard said: "It's not where you take things from - it's where you take them to."

- Jim Jarmusch

3D

RAE LEONARD

STATE FAIR; CHILDHOOD'S END

1970

My parents took me to the New York State Fair in Syracuse the summer I was turning four. They were young and splitting up, ill-equipped for marriage and parenting, maybe subconsciously they were trying to lose me there. They had stopped at the restrooms. They both dropped my hand and went around two different sides of the building, assuming the other one had me. I found the animal tent. I was a mop top of red hair wearing a pink dress with a white collar, wandering about in my anklet socks and patent leather shoes, I took in prize winning 4-H horses, cows, rabbits and pigs. Their teenage owners primped and gussied up the animals, giving them the treatment like Dorothy and her friends got before they were ushered in to see the wizard.

I stayed for what seemed like a long while. I didn't reach out and pet them as other children were doing. I was afraid to attract attention to myself, afraid I would cry. I stood touching them from a distance, arms folded over my belly, alternatively switching to a solid stance with my hands on my hips, like dads do at the beach, looking out onto the horizon.

I moved on with intent through the food court. I wasn't distracted by the families at picnic tables eating fried chicken, corn on the cob and candied apples. I had other places to be, like the big building in front of me. Leaving the hustle and bustle behind, I entered inside where it was quiet like a museum or a church. Shiny plows and all kinds of choppers and trucks were on display. I climbed up on the red tractor with a plush brown leather seat and a big shiny mustard colored steering wheel to hang on to. I was now enjoying the view from my high perch. In my mind's eye I saw my dad finding me before he actually did. I saw him walking toward me, spotting me, his brow softening as the great weight lifted from his shoulders.

I wasn't afraid because I knew he would find me, I saw it before it happened. I saw my mother too. She had already resigned herself to one of the unspeakable scenarios that she had played in her head. She was sitting comatose on a bench while police searched for me and I knew she would be fine when my dad brought me back on his shoulders.

Now my dad opened the big doors to the exhibition hall. He walked into the building scanning the floor far below me. Finally his eyes reached higher and he saw me. "Where were you Daddy? You were lost."

Clairvoyance - Clear Vision

A clairvoyant person receives pictures in the form of images, mini-movies, glimpses, dreams or visions. Images can be literal or metaphorical.

Afterward, my parents took me to a Howard Johnson for dinner. From my booster seat I ordered spaghetti and meatballs. My mother said, "Well, there goes that dress." I refused to hang a paper napkin from my collar. As I twirled bite after bite of pasta onto my fork, I lifted my napkin from my lap and blotted the corners of my mouth. When I was finished, I crossed my fork and spoon and laid them on my plate. There was not one spatter of sauce on my dress. She was wrong and I was on my own now.

KETCHUP AND MUSTARD

1979 - 1983

"To be young is to be as one of The Immortals."

–W.C Hazlitt

I was a latchkey kid in the East Village who started smoking and drinking with my friends when I was twelve. This was before NYU spread east over the neighborhood, before the Yuppies who brought shops and cafes. Alphabet City was burnt out buildings, abandoned cars, bodegas and junkies. Mama and I didn't get on well so she spent weekends at her boyfriend's place, leaving her apartment open to become the weekend party spot. I would phone my friends' parents, impersonate my mother and reassuringly invite my friends over for chaperoned board games and a popcorn sleepover.

We were a tight bunch of kids, members of an elite choral group headed by our brilliant musical director, Dr. Sharon. He pulled the best out of each and everyone of us, shining us up to showcase our unique gifts. We toured the city singing and dancing in hotels and recording commercials like *"I Love New York."* We were talented and wild, getting out of class a lot. I had a good ear and I loved to sing, yet was often plagued with congestion and sore throats caused by my self-doubt and poor diet.

Clairaudience - Clear Hearing

A clairaudient person retains information best when they hear it spoken aloud. They may have natural talent in their auditory faculties, often becoming a musician, singer, writer or public speaker. They may hear ringing, high-pitched sounds, music or thoughts spoken aloud in their own or someone else's voice. These messages can come from spirit guides or those who have passed on.

I had strong intuitive senses although they were starting to get clouded with alcohol and weed. I knew things about teachers, the lady sitting in the park, the guy who owned the bodega. I knew who I could trust and who I would disarm so I could make a quick getaway. At school, I stayed under the radar as much as possible. I was ashamed of not really having a family and I didn't like to show teachers I was bright. It was easier to be bored than risk more being expected from me. Being invisible would help me slide into a place setting at a friend's dinner table or squeeze into their station wagon for a beach day.

My friends and I would cross 7th St and climb through the brambles at the entrance into Tompkins Square Park, to cop nickel bags of seedy brown dirt weed. Then we would hit the liquor store on the corner for a jug of syrupy Gallo wine, which obviously wasn't considered alcohol in those days as they sold it to children. Back up the five flights of stairs to my mother's tenement apartment, we mixed the wine with orange juice and coined it *Tropicgallo*. It had an iridescent pink hue when you puked it up.

The word got out and older kids started showing up, taking over the living room and my mother's bedroom, panting, grinding. My friends and I found ourselves confined to the kitchen. We concocted batches of ketchup, mustard, eggs and poured it out the window onto people's laundry hanging in the courtyard below.

The sink got pulled out of the wall, too many kids sitting on it and oops my mom got evicted. The next thing I knew I was sent to live with an aunt in Squaresville, New York. She taught me how to run a household, how to cook and clean, fold laundry – I felt these chores had been passed down from my grandmother and great grandmothers who passed before I was born. "The kitchen is not clean after dinner until we sweep the floor!", they echoed.

I didn't hate it there but I felt a bit like a stray cat they found on their front porch. I probably would've stayed longer had my aunt's creepy husband not taken an interest in my wardrobe. First taking me shopping for new clothes, then coming into my bedroom downstairs with his weird Moroccan liqueur, wanting me to try on my new clothes for him. I saw where this was going. I called my dad and told him to come pick me up. He said he was bringing a baseball bat "to teach that guy a lesson." He pulled into the driveway on the weekend. I spied a Wiffle Bat in the back seat. One of the side windows in the car was missing and there was a RAMBO movie poster in its place. I thought the poster was an attempt at intimidation but I found out later it was simply the right size piece of cardboard to cover the missing window. After coffee, pastries and awkward conversation, I packed my new clothes into the car. No one was surprised when the Chevy Impala wouldn't start. *Creepy Uncle* had it towed to a garage before he gave us a ride to the bus station. He held my face still as he planted a wet kiss on my lips. "Bye Baby," he said.

I gave up on high school while living with my dad upstate. I felt like the house was getting kinda crowded, between him, a bunch of kids, his wife, AND his girlfriend, who was also living there at the time. I missed the scene in the city and just kept getting this nagging feeling I should blow town. I said to my dad's girlfriend with her big boobs and crazy ice blue eyes, "I think I'm going to head back to the city." She was standing with the fridge door open eating a tub of macaroni salad from the supermarket, keeping her eyes on me like a wild animal protecting her food. I hitched a ride to the city and it turned out to be a good move to split when I did. The house burned down soon after.

Claircognizance - Clear Knowing

Everyone has gut feelings. This is when we have a hunch or knowledge of people or events we would not normally have knowledge of. Impressions simply pop into our minds. It could be a premonition, a forewarning of something happening in the future. Maybe something in a dream pops up in waking life. Claircognizance requires courage and faith because often there is no practical explanation as to why we suddenly 'know' things. Philosophers, scientists, professors, spiritual leaders and salespeople tend to be highly intuitive and seem to know things with a sense of certainty. These people have claircognizance as one of their dominant senses.

SUMMER CAMP

1979

One lucky summer, my aunt and uncle sent me to a ritzy theater camp. They signed me up for every session as I had nothing else to do and I'm sure they thought it wise to keep me off the streets. On the rowdy bus ride to camp I observed the other kids. Trying to impress my seatmate, I told her things.

"That boy with the big mouth will calm down when we get to camp, he just gets loud when he is nervous. That girl's parents are getting divorced. She lives on the Upper West Side and has an old cat that she is worried to leave for the summer." Another girl was eating Junior Mints, "Oh, she has a suitcase full of those."

All was good fun as I just got feelings about people. Moving around a lot as a kid and basically raising myself I learned to read people super-fast. I sensed their feelings, sometimes their thoughts and I knew how they would react. It was a survival mechanism that allowed me to suss up people and situations quickly.

Clairsentience - Clear Sensing
A clairsentient person can sense people's feelings and is not distracted by what others are saying. They can physically and emotionally pick up on environmental stimuli and energy being generated from those around them. They may know things that have not been revealed.

The seasonal program was dazzling and ambitious. The productions overlapped and I juggled some fabulous roles. As Rosalind in Shakespeare's comedy, *As You Like It*, I dressed as a man in a green forestry cap, short camel bloomers and red tights. As May Rose Cottage, in Dylan Thomas' *Under Milkwood*, I was a 17-year-old-never-been-kissed seductress, daydreaming and lounging on a hill barely clothed. Wearing a seaman's blue and white striped shirt and white sailor pants, I sailed in Gilbert and Sullivan's musical, *HMS Pinafore*. I wanted to play Buttercup but I am no soprano. I championed as the tragic Appalachian gal, Barbara Allen in *Dark of the Moon* wearing a deep rust colored dress with tiny shimmering gold buttons.

My biggest challenge was offstage. I was an inner city kid while the other campers had monogrammed trunks, attended private schools and received lavish care packages from *Balducci's* and *Rumplemyers*. I felt out of my league.

The girl with the junior mints reported some of her stash missing and I was the prime suspect. It was a whole offstage drama which began with a bunk sitdown, and me being accused of stealing the candy, continued with an emotional snort in my defense, "I don't even like Junior Mints!", and concluded with a narrow escape as I slammed the cabin door behind me. Although I was innocent of stealing the candy, my enviousness was clearly palpable and I sensed this showdown was borne of my own insecurities.

I left camp with some serious theater chops by way of the infirmary after I had joined the junior counselors drinking moonshine by a campfire. I learned not to run my mouth off and went underground with my *knowings*. I implemented a new strategic plan. Operation: Kill Pain / Fit In.

THE VEIL IS LIFTED AT SHOPRITE

1985

Sharon Gannon was my Sunday morning yoga teacher at the gym on Lafayette St. She's a vegan animal rights activist, yogini queen and I idolized her. This was before she and David Life opened The Jivamukti Yoga Center which catapulted yoga into a worldwide sensation.

I decided to go vegetarian and when I told my mother she said, "I am not surprised."

"Really Mom? Why?"

"When you were a toddler in a cart at Shoprite, I wheeled you past the meat counter and you started shrieking and burst into tears."

I recalled the swinging doors behind the meat counter being wide open and the butcher standing beside monstrous carcasses that hung from the ceiling on giant hooks, wielding his cleaver, wearing a blood-stained white coat.

"You were inconsolable," she told me, and asked, "Well dolly, where did you think meat came from?"

"The drug store!" I wailed.

I had always thought my answer was a random quirky toddler comment, a punchline that lightened up an upsetting event in my life until many years later when I screened David Whitehead's documentary, *Cult of the Medics.* The film reveals the occult history of the medical industrial complex and why medical authorities, doctors, pharmacists and butchers all wear the same white coats. I had connected the two coats together many, many moons before. The remark was actually a claircognizant observation.

A WOMAN'S RIGHT TO
CHOOSE IS PATRIARCHAL
NEWSPEAK BULLSHIT

1986

I'm in a tenement building in the East Village. It's 3 a.m. Two guys and I are scrounging around a flat's filthy floor, teeth chattering, searching for alleged bits of fallen cocaine. For the past few hours, we've been smoking from this grimy glass pipe, I am no longer having a good time, the room reeks like poison gas and I am ready to split but I feel obligated to help them look.

A cook who I worked with at Yaffa Cafe, invited me over to some guy's apartment to freebase after our shift ended. The cook got an eight ball, 300 dollars worth of cocaine and he didn't even ask me to chip in. How could I miss this opportunity? This wasn't crack, the raging, super-addictive street drug that was all the rage with the hollow-eyed zombies. This was an extravagant, exclusive drug. The cocaine was vaporized with a special flame to purify it. This must be a really good high since he spent three shifts of pay at Yaffa's for it.

We went to his friend's flat to partake as he had all the accoutrements. The building was being renovated. The whole Lower East Side was being gentrified and this building was no exception. Six story walk ups, originally built in the 19th century for poor immigrants, were now being chopped up, cleaned up and the rents quadrupled. The hallway was littered with new construction debris powdered with a layer of sheetrock dust. Mixed with piss, it made a distinctly unique odor, *The Sweet Smell of Piss and Progress*, though this flat was just another East Village dump. All the woodwork and cabinets were covered with a vile gray paint. I scored a few bits of dust and I think a piece of uncooked pasta to contribute to the next pile of coke. I swigged another Rolling Rock because gee, I wasn't tired at all and after declining another hit of what they were now smoking, I hit the streets. My Billy Martin cowboy boots with real spurs on the back, clicked on sidewalks as ripped up as my fishnet stockings. With the late spring breeze enveloping me with little whirlwinds of garbage, I thought, "I should kill myself, or maybe I should go to Martha's Vineyard."

I had been to the island when I was fifteen with a friend and her kind family who rented a house for the summer when I was fifteen. It was a summer colony for New Englanders, picturesque harbor towns and sandy beaches, the opposite of the East Village.

I called my dad, "Wanna drive me to Martha's Vineyard?"

He didn't ask about my plans or if I had any money, he just said, "OK."

Gotta love him. I packed a bag, all my stuff,

ditched out on my job, and my dad picked me up in a *Hail Mary* of a car. We made it to Woods Hole just in time to slip onto the last ferry. Aboard the boat, my hair and lungs drank in the ocean mist as my heart softened with the company of families going on summer vacation. We made it, Virgo Me and Pisces Pops. Like peas and carrots, we were on our way.

Once we were on the island my spirits sank as quickly as the sun was setting. We hadn't thought to make a reservation anywhere and it was Memorial Day weekend. Didn't we know that? F*ck. We were nothing like those families on the ferry who had packed chicken salad sandwiches with walnuts and grapes and houses to go to. I tried not to panic. Tired and hungry, we knocked on doors of pastel-colored Victorian houses with B&B signs, in the town of Oak Bluffs.

We were quite the sight, a scruffy dude and his daughter. Old ladies gaped at my teased hair, black eyeliner, and rubber mini skirt. "You know it's Memorial Day weekend?" Yes, we knew.

We knocked on one more pink door. A professor from NYU took pity on us and let us sleep in an alcove. The next morning my dad took me to breakfast at a coffee shop, gave me all the money he had and left. It was enough to pay for the alcove for a few more days. I started panicking again. Maybe I should just leave now while I still had the money to get off the island. *"Damn, I need a job."* I smoked a joint and held down a stinging panic as I slipped on my one piece of clothing that wasn't black, a white cotton onesie, from the forties. Officially lingerie and a size too big so it wasn't skin tight. With my western belt cinched around my waist it resembled a jumpsuit. I hit clam shacks, souvenir shops, and the movie theater – no luck. I sat on the pier and watched boaty people on their boats. They were laughing as their vessels swayed and their cocktail glasses clinked.

I walked back to the inn and sat on a swing on the front porch. I pulled out a roach and lit it. Smoking didn't make me feel any better, just dull and gross.

Professor Innkeeper came out on the porch and asked, "Are you smoking pot!?" Both speechless, we stared at each other. Finally he said, "You can't smoke pot here," and left shaking his head.

An annoying boy came up onto the porch. "Do you smell weed?," he asked. He was staying at the inn, but his friend left suddenly and he was stuck paying for the whole room himself. I asked him how much he was paying and it was just a bit more than my alcove. I bummed a cigarette and made him a proposition. I would move into his room and split the cost with him. He didn't need much convincing. I went inside and thanked *Professor Innkeeper* for the lodging and told him I was moving to *Annoying Boy's* room, effective immediately. He said, "Well that's not exactly how it works around here." I ignored him and got my bag and moved it to the top floor of the Victorian.

I had cut my expenses in half and now even had a view of the harbor. Only problem now was *Annoying Boy*. He invited me to the local dive bar with him and even though I wanted a beer badly, I said "You go ahead Dave, I need to unpack."

"Doug," he said. Whatever. I locked the door behind him. I set up a bed for him on the floor using a pillow and a blanket and climbed into the big brass bed with my silent movie picture book. Now I kind of wished I had gone to the bar with him. I bet he would have bought me a beer and a bag of Lay's chips, the ones clipped on those metal stands behind the bar. My stomach grumbled. I got up and unlocked the door and climbed back in bed. He came in drunk later and looked at me incredulously, "I didn't think you would really be here."

"There is your bed Darren, don't forget to brush your teeth," I gestured to the floor.

"Oh, come on," he said, trying to sit on the bed.

I spat, "You back away this instant or I'll scream bloody murder."

He backed off grumbling, then settled in on the floor, punching his pillow.

The next day I didn't even look for a job. I took the bus to Vineyard Haven and went to The Black Dog for a bowl of $11 lobster bisque. I was wearing a vintage dusty rose lace dress with black velvet trim, ripped up fishnet stockings and my prized Billy Martins. I had seen them on an *Uptown Girl* at a bar. I complimented her and I asked where she had gotten them.

"Billy Martin's," she tossed her fine blond hair.

"Oh cool, thanks."

What the hell was Billy Martin's? I asked around. It was an upscale cowboy store on Madison Ave. I had saved my shekels for them and actually went *above* 14th Street to buy them. I justified the purchase by saying they would be my only footwear, and they were.

As I walked down Circuit Avenue in Oak Bluffs, I saw two cool kids about my age staring at me from across the street. Tim was tall with ducktail hair, clam diggers, a vintage shirt and two-tone suede shoes. Peg had a bleached blond pixie, a pencil skirt and flats.

We gravitated toward each other until we were talking. They were from Tyler, an art school in Philly and we listened to the new *Nick Cave and The Bad Seeds* cassette on their Walkman. They worked at the Wesley Hotel, a big white old Victorian gal right on the harbor. They took me over there to meet the manager who hired me to work the night shift at the front desk with Peg. It was a perfect job because the ferries didn't run at night so no one was actually ever checking in. Every night I slept on one of the couches in the lobby while Peg manned the desk in case something happened, which never did. They invited me to move into their room, which was a tiny garret with one bed, but Peg and I worked nights and Tim washed the hotel laundry by day, so only having one bed was never a problem. Besides, he was gay anyway.

Peg also worked by day at the hip vintage clothing store on the island. She took me there and Barry, the bald, short-tempered, beady-eyed owner hired me. The shop was the island celebrity mecca, with James Taylor, Carly Simon, Jim Belushi, and Dan Aykroyd stopping by all the time. There was a lounge upstairs with a bar and pool table and I got to make drinks for Barry and his friends. And the clothes ... I picked out a Swedish motorcycle cop's leather jacket, a straw hat from the 40's with a big green sash that probably came from Katherine Hepburn's head, a smoking hot tennis outfit from the 60's and an armful of bakelite bracelets. Barry wouldn't allow his lowly employees purchase his carefully curated collection slated for his celebrity customers. So I would buy them when he was away on shopping trips to Boston. I spent all my summer money on vintage one-of-a-kind pieces which I couldn't wear out and about in fear he would spot me. When he returned from his trips he would be very curious who bought his prized garments.

One rare day off, I took the bus to Edgartown and was walking by shop windows when I could have sworn I saw *On Again Off Again Boyfriend* riding bikes with a brunette girl, coming straight toward me. SH*T. It couldn't possibly be him. No way was he riding bikes with a girl in Edgartown when he was at State University, in Upstate NY. Oh blow me, it was summer vacation! He was right on top of me and almost impaled me with his front wheel.

We were always doing this, *literally* running into each other. Last time it was in the Village about five months earlier, during an "off again". Spotting each other in front of Panchitos, we hesitantly grabbed margaritas, tumbled into bed at my place, and he was gone on an early bus to catch his classes.

He looked good in Edgartown, wearing a t-shirt, shorts, and boat sneakers, but still edgy, not a complete freak, like me. Shock. Small talk. Awkward. He pulled his bike away from me, playing it cool since he was with someone. He said he had taken a job at a golf course on the island for the summer and this was a girl he worked with. Whatever. I told him where to find me and I expected him to show up at my door the next day but he didn't. Well, I had been the one to ruin our relationship. When we met he was 17 from New Jersey. I was 6 months older and a city kid who knew more about music and drugs and all the important things. He was super smart and a talented artist. I was wild and nowhere near ready to settle down in a relationship. Our thing was undeniably special, yet, I denied it.

A few days passed. Since I couldn't wear any of my new clothes around town, I was lounging in my vintage tennis outfit in our tiny, stifling attic room. I unsnapped the top button on my skort. They were unusually tight, why? Ugh. No more beers for me. Suddenly something fluttered in my stomach. Weird. Another flutter. Really weird.

"What's wrong with you?" asked Peg.

"Come put your hand here." She put her hand on my belly. "Just wait."

Flutter … flutter.

"What have you got in there, an alien? You'd better go see a doctor."

I took off the next day and went to the Mid-Island Clinic.

"When was your last period?"

"Like, a year ago, maybe … I've been depressed." They took tests.

"You're over five months pregnant."

"Can I have an abortion?"

"It is too late for that."

Wow. I was catapulted into a higher dimension. *No more 3D disconnection.* I was in a gateway. I felt exhilarated and empowered to be carrying a life inside me. I had a purpose. I was now a creator. Shockingly, like a bolt of lightning, my life had meaning.

Now I just needed a plan. I'll call my drag-queen-girlfriend, Sista, when I get back to the hotel. She'll be at the Boy Bar on St. Marks, where she'd often let me dance on the bar for tips on lesbian night. I could move in with her and she'll help me raise the baby. I was sure of it.

I wouldn't ask *On Again Off Again* for anything. I would just tell him, "I am raising our child, alone." *That* should make him feel horrible for being a lowly college kid, one who can't even marry me and get us a little house in the countryside, like the one in *A Room with a View*.

Whoa, Nellie. Had I been with anyone else? I searched my memory of drunken nights five months ago, not an easy or palatable task. Oh ... well, yeah ... there was *Rude Boy From London*. He had come home with me one night after last call at the Milk Bar on 7th Ave South. I had seen him a few times after that evening and thankfully he acted like there was nothing memorable between us, because there wasn't. I was just a place to shoot his heroin. Probably, hopefully, he didn't even remember the incident, as he lacked some faculties, as well as some teeth, due to heavy drug use. I shuddered and put this distasteful recollection back into the vault, probably, hopefully for good.

The next night, *On Again Off Again* and I were sitting on the employee picnic table next to the dumpsters, drinking a six-pack of Rolling Rocks at the Wesley Hotel. I told him. He got up to leave.

"Don't you want to finish the sixer?"

"No." he said.

I called Sista, "Don't be ridiculous, you're not going to RAISE this child, you are going to SELL IT. Now listen to me, you're a gorgeous girl, you are gonna get an apartment and a ton of cash out of this, at least. I will hook you up with my lawyer, we work together on insurance cases." What did that even mean? I wondered. I found out it means she and another guy, in cahoots with her lawyer, were pulling insurance scams. They faked car accidents by cracking up cars, giving each other black eyes and slamming their bodies against dashboards, hoping to break bones.

I came back to the city and went to stay with her. Holding the phone between her chin and shoulder, she called her lawyer. With her meaty hands and inch-and-a-half acrylic nails, she opened a can of chicken noodle soup for me and the baby.

His downtown office was as shoddy as his practice. At least he really was a lawyer, although I had my doubts. He came around in front of the desk with a notepad and took down all the details. My age, 20, my heritage, Irish and Lithuanian. Did I smoke? Use drugs? No and no. Father's heritage?

"My father?"

"No, the baby's father."

"Oh. Italian."

"Let's say English."

"OK," I went along.

He told me he had a family who would be interested in adopting the baby. They would get me an apartment for the rest of my pregnancy and there would be an adoption fee in it for me. But first I needed to go see a doctor. Did I have a doctor? Actually, I had seen my mother's gynecologist a few times..

"Just go get a physical."

I called the doctor's office and the receptionist asked me the reason for the visit. I said, nonchalantly, "I am having a baby and I need a check up." The gynecologist, *Doctor Handsome*, had an office on the Upper East Side. He examined me, then asked me to meet him in his brown leathery office.

He asked me point blank, "Why are you having this baby?"

I broke down in big wet gasping sobs. In a flash I saw

my future, how difficult and complicated my life would become as a young single mother, how disadvantaged my child would be.

"I don't know, they told me it's too late to have an abortion."

"This is New York and the cutoff is five and a half months. I will say you qualify and I'm scheduling you in tomorrow, 7 a.m. at the clinic. "

I was handed a piece of paper with an address and walked outside. My mother was standing there under a plaque, "Dr. Hanson, OB/GYN."

That night I stopped sweet-talking to the baby. I turned my back on the little tyke completely. The next morning my mother took me in a cab to the clinic. When we pulled up, people with bad skin and serial killer glasses, who looked like they had crawled out from under rocks, surrounded the cab. They were yelling and pushing posters of bloody fetuses dumped in garbage pails in my face. My mother held on to me and led me through.

Once inside, I was told I was having a two day procedure called a Dilation and Evacuation, a D&E. They would insert these spongy stints into my cervix which would expand overnight, dilating me so that my uterus could be suctioned out the next day. Oy. This was a whole thing, like a whole big baby thing they had to get out of me.

Afterwards, we got takeout Chinese and went back to my mother's apartment. When she went to run some errands, I popped open a beer and called Sista who seethed, "You little fool! You just have to make it three more months for all that money!"

I thought of all the drugs I took in the past six

months and said that I just wanted it all behind me now and no baby to think of for the rest of my life.

I ate broccoli and tofu on the pull-out sofa and dozed. My stomach started turning over badly. The phone rang, I let the answering machine pick up as it wasn't my apartment and it couldn't be for me. I heard the lawyer's voice talking to me. SH*T. Sista must have given him this number. I picked up as I didn't want the message being recorded on my mother's machine.

"What are you doing?! We had a deal. You signed a contract!"

Did I? Maybe I did. I told him that I was sorry but I changed my mind.

"What you are doing is illegal!"

I hung up on him. I was in big pain now. My mother came back and put warm compresses on my belly. There was no rest for her that night as there was nowhere to sleep other than the pull-out on which I was writhing.

Next morning, past the mole people, I am in a queue with other girls in hospital gowns on gurneys. Separated by shame, none of us talked to each other. They knock me out by injection.

When I wake up, things have happened, a big pad between my legs. I am bleeding but attended to, like in an army hospital after a battle. They pass out cookies and juice. I am grateful to fill myself with them as I am now empty.

I called my dad and told him. I heard a high-pitched wail that sounded like a cry from our ancestors who had been saddened by this fiasco. I denied myself the grieving process. I didn't deserve to grieve, did I? I felt relieved, didn't I? This had been my choice, hadn't it? I sunk my disputing emotions with shots of whiskey.

HEROIN AND THE LAW OF ATTRACTION

2004

"Her–o–in…it's my wife and it's my life."

–The Velvet Underground

I started listening to Abraham Hicks on an old boom box in my kitchen that still had a cassette player in it. I grabbed a bunch of tapes from a free box at The Omega Institute when I did my yoga teacher training and was working my way through them while I drank wine and made dinner for my family.

Jerry Hicks would ask his wife, Esther questions, and Abraham, a group of non-sentient beings who she channeled, would answer through her. They explained how your emotions are your guide to all the things you desire and if you are feeling bad, ain't none of them going to happen. The trick, according to Abe, is to get your emotions perpetually rolling in a positive direction and all the things you imagine will roll unto you.

I was *superburnt*. A wife and a mother with

two young children. The routine and demands of the nuclear unit was a grind. I was more suited to raising a family in a communal environment but hubby was not on board. Parenting, cooking, cleaning, shopping, organizing, driving, as well as preparing and teaching my own yoga classes, I developed a pernicious wine habit to take the edge off.

One day it whispered to me, "You know what you need?"

"What?"

"Some heroin."

A natural substance, it was from the seed pod of poppies. It came from flowers. It was *natural*. They named it *Heroin*, like a heroine, a female hero. Who cares that it's an opioid drug made from morphine, developed and coined by the Bayer Pharmaceutical Company in 1874.

Alcohol just wasn't cutting it for me anymore. I wanted to drift away on the clouds, to completely Blot Out. To Rest. Just plain ME TIME. I had gone through a minor heroin phase when I was young, just snorting, who didn't in the East Village? I wasn't afraid of it. It wasn't the devil for gosh sakes, people made such a big deal about it. I wasn't stupid, I'd never shoot it. But where the heck would I score some heroin in my mom routine, on the yoga studio circuit, living in the Hudson Valley? Wait. *Ask and it is Given*, as Abraham says. All I had to do was happily expect it and keep my spirits high, keep focused on the positive aspect of everything and the Universe must deliver. It's a Law.

A couple of days later I pulled into the library parking lot to rest a little before pickup time at the kids' Waldorf School, when an old junkie came to my car window. I couldn't believe it. Junkies were not common sights in my sleepy mountain town. He wasn't like a stoop kid, he was like a disheveled writer, an intellectual junk, just my type.

"Hi, have you got a dollar? I'm a little short on my library fines."

This was too good to be true.

"Sure," I handed him ten dollars, his eyes widened, "no problem. Hey, do you know where I can get some H?"

"H? Why would a girl like you want *that*? No way, why would you ask me? Do I look like I would know where to get that?" His hands rubbing the crisp ten dollar bill.

I let him think.

"Well maybe I might know somebody, I don't know."

I was writing my number on a piece of paper, "My name is Carol. If you happen to come across some, call me."

"OK, Carol."

I forgot all about the encounter until I got a call weeks later. Before I picked up I knew exactly who it was and went out onto the back porch. I gazed at the hammock I had set up between two ash trees. *Muppet Crew* had knotted and gnarled it, using it to spin each other around until one of the muppets got hurt.

"Carol? I got what you are looking for."

A wave of euphoria pulsed through me from my Svadhisthana Chakra, from my lower belly. The feeling of scoring drugs is like setting a date when you are in a new romance. Pure anticipation. A pre-high with no crash or side effects.

We met back at our spot behind the library. This time I had *Muppet Crew* in the back seat. I pulled into the parking lot and parked a bit away from him.

"I will be right back guys."

Chit-chat. He handed me a bag that felt right to me. I handed him an envelope that felt right to him. Just a casual exchange built on mutual trust. Trust in the universe.

I got back in the car. Shoot. Why didn't I get his number? Oh. He called me so I had his number in my new Blackberry. Not that I knew how to use it, but I'd figure it out.

"Who was that?" *Muppet Crew* was curious.

"Who? Oh that was my friend... Link. Who wants to go to the park?"

I opened the bag when we got home. Three little crinkly paper packages with a blue stamp on them that read, BOSCO. Ohhh why didn't I get more? So flipping cool. I put the packets in my kitchen drawer. My newly renovated kitchen was now complete. Something special was coming. A joy ride just for me. A soft pillowy dream world where nothing was expected of me. Relief.

A juice box straw cut in half. A compact mirror. A razor blade. It was all coming together. I locked myself in the bathroom after I put *Muppet Show* to bed. Pour. Chop. Sniff. Whiskey chaser for good measure. Clean up thoroughly. I lay down. Deep relaxation wafting over me. Nothing would ever bother me again.

Date night came and we dropped the *Muppet Crew* off for a sleepover at friends. I told *hubby* I got the stuff from our druggie friend. He pretended to be interested in it. He wasn't but he liked the way I got very relaxed.

Like a ragdoll.

"How much of that stuff do you have?

"Not enough."

When it was all gone I called Link's number. The phone was disconnected.

MY VACATION

2014

Close to the end of my forty year love affair with alcohol and drugs, I went to see the gynecologist, now known as *Ol' Doc Handsome*. I got undressed quickly, freezing in a sterile bright fluorescent eerily soundproof box. Then the wait, isolated and awkward, anticipating the door to open and to be greeted by a busy stressed man who had a few short moments to give to me, most of which were spent with my legs spread. Out to the receptionist, did my insurance go through? I hope so. Did I owe money? I hope not. The whole experience, stressful. Doctor visits had nothing to do with healing and health for me. Why did I still go? Well, I was in a tailspin in my life, not taking care of myself, not really thinking clearly and the nurse had called, guilting me into my yearly check up.

The same nurse called me after my visit and told me to come in to talk about my pap smear. I was not nervous or fearful, I was annoyed. Oh right, I remembered now, you go to a doctors office for a check up, they find something wrong and now you are hooked into a cycle of tests, prescriptions, procedures, billing etc.

Ol' Doc said I had precancerous cells on my cervix.

"What does that mean?"

He said that some of the cells on my cervix were not healthy and MAY turn cancerous. I felt a zap of shame emanating from Svadhisthana. My cervix wasn't up to snuff.

He repeated himself like a bad salesman, "They may not turn into cancer, but they may."

I had read that pap smears are not a smear taken on your cervix as the name implies, that actually doctors use a small brush or spatula that causes a nick on your cervix. This in turn causes your body to create abnormal cells in this spot, hence the test creates the problem. I kept my mouth shut. Why had I even allowed him to examine me? What was I doing here? The whole thing was barbaric. An in-office procedure was recommended. He would go into my vagina with that instrument of torture, the antiquated, icy metal speculum, and lop off the dirty, undesirable part of my cervix with a scalpel. Ya, there had to be alternatives. Aren't there supplements I could take? Green drinks? Vaginal suppositories with herbs in them? Something else before cranking me open and taking a scalpel to my Whohaa?" I was too polluted to ask these healthful questions. Instead, I saw my angle.

"How long would I need to rest after the procedure?"

"Three or four days."

"Would I be in a lot of pain?"

"I will prescribe painkillers."

Bingo. That's what I wanted to hear. Sign me up

baby. Three to four days of bedrest? Painkillers? I would have considered taking the tip of my left pinky off to get a break and blot out my life for a few days.

I knew the whole thing was a racket. From the disturbing, humiliating pap smear, to slicing off a hunk of my cervix, this process was designed for business, white coats, and butchering business. Health Care! Come in for tests so we can find something to cut out and get you on pharmaceuticals to keep you docile, sick and compliant. "Well, I would turn this around to my advantage," thought my warped booze-brain. I was being clever, carving out some down time for myself with painkillers. I didn't see that I was once again complying to knives in my womb. This was the best I could hope for at the time, someone else telling me what to do with my body when my soul was sick.

GOOD GOLLY MISS MOLLY
AND THE END

2018

"Everything in moderation, even moderation."

–Oscar Wilde

One night I was out on the back deck of a local hot spot. I was pretty wasted, a cocktail in one hand when someone handed me a joint. I looked up and saw a young yoga student of mine staring at me. My face flushed.

"What a hypocrite," I thought to myself, "I can't do this anymore."

I quit teaching yoga. I stopped helping people and went back into entertainment, a great booze-brain decision. I stumbled back into acting, mostly booking jobs as broken down alcoholics like in *Detachment* with Adrian Brody. I could smoke and drink all in the name of research for my roles.

My ten year old said, "Mom, you play such great crack whores."

"Gee thanks, kid."

Druggie Friend scored a whole bunch of MDMA, aka Molly. He said his friend was a chemist and made it in a pop-up lab. That sounded dubious but I didn't care. I stocked up. I started taking just a little toot most days as a boost and an appetite suppressant. Molly is so good but a bit speedy so I drank to balance out the high. I found I could get away with some appetizers and then just drink until I passed out. I stayed thin. Actresses can never be too thin.

Whatever problems *Hubby* and I had, I'm sure my drinking contributed to them. When we separated, my teenagers resented me.

One weekend their dad went on a business trip so I stopped by to see if the teenagers wanted to get some dinner with me. They acted cool toward me as usual, but something else was going on. After refusing my offer, they couldn't wait to get rid of me. I went to the bathroom, took a little bump and decided to hang around for a while. Sure enough, some of their girlfriends showed up with booze.

I knew most of these girls since my kids were in grade school. I had a drink with them and thought, well, I can supervise this party, no problem. A couple of more drinks and the boys started showing up. I began losing control as I stood at the door playing *Drunk-mom Doorman* as more and more kids showed up. Trying to throw boys out as they were dodging past me, the girls screamed in protest, "you're kicking out our boyfriends!" Kids started puking outside, a boy passed out in the driveway and when I went to check on him, I saw two cop cars sitting across the street in the middle school parking lot.

I ran into the house and announced, "the cops are here!"

The place cleared out fast. I had some boys peel the kid off the driveway on their way out and shove him in the back of one of their cars. Miraculously, and I still cannot comprehend how, the cops didn't notice the bacchanal full of underage kids right across the street.

My world was getting narrower and narrower. I was plagued with guilt, shame and intense neck and shoulder pain. Acting jobs dried up. Alcohol, molly, painkillers, weed, and now, burgers. Strangely, I had started craving animal flesh to wash down the booze.

A guy I had a crush on asked, "Do you drink every night?" That stung. No one had ever questioned my drinking before. I started to hide it. I had a toot and a drink before we went out. Why wait and have to talk to people before I found the bar? This was also cost effective as well as I now had financial problems. I started hiding booze in cabinets so I didn't have to hold the telltale glass in my hand. This led to guzzling wine bottles in the bathroom. I had a nip of wine before I went out on errands to take the edge off. A glass of wine or two with lunch and then a catnap. Isn't that what Europeans do? Sometimes I was too sloshed to even make it out of the house on errands. This was practical as it also saved money.

A friend who had a condo on Miami Beach invited my daughter and I on a vacation. We actually had a fantastic time. We hit the nightlife hard and nursed hangovers with mimosas on the beach. She was under age yet no one questioned her because she was with us.

We were extremely lucky that the *Alcohol Demons* never showed up to mess with us. When we got back to New York, I had a moment of clarity. I got down on my knees and thanked the demons for sparing us on this trip. Things could have gone very differently. I knew that the wildly charmed alcohol drenched trip they allowed us was a trap laid for me. They would get me next time, I was sure of it.

Funny how my whole life I had kind of a handle on my drinking and then one day I no longer did. Now at any event or party where booze was free-flowing, I got wasted and blacked out followed by slivering, immobilizing hangovers. At a party, I fell down the stairs outside the house. FLUMP. I gashed my forehead open on a rock. I hid for a week to avoid, "What happened to you?!?" I flopped off the bar stool at my dad's seventy-fifth birthday party and had to be carried to the car. I drove drunk. I lost keys. I lost wallets. I lost my keen sense of smell.

I had played hard for 40 years with booze, now it was playing hard with me. I could hear a dark entity whispering in my ear, telling me I needed the booze, needed the drugs. I knew it was a lie. No, people led extraordinary and happy lives without it. But who would I be without these wickedly enchanting props and crutches? Well, I would find out.

This explicit insight, this consciousness I had to override society's programming, to override my subconscious self-hatred and neglect, led me out of addiction. It was just a glimmer, a crack of light through a curtain, a wisp of clarity that allowed me to see there was something else involved in my decision making.

People often ask me how I quit. I wasn't living in

a fleabag hotel, I wasn't court-ordered or confronted by my family and forced into rehab. I was just a classic under-achieving girl with a drinking problem. Even though I had not hit rock bottom, I decided to stop digging. I knew that the drugs were fueled by the alcohol and that by exorcizing the booze demon I would render the other drugs powerless. My plan of attack was subtle. I would not announce a battle but I would quietly prepare for one. I would appear nonchalant while plotting my exit strategy, continuing to drink and to be able to say my goodbyes. Even I didn't know the date of my escape.

I leaned into my Buddhist and yoga practices before I sneakily pulled the rug out from under the bottle. I started listening to sober podcasts. My playlist: *Anxiety and Alcohol: The Vicious Cycle, Ten Things That Happened When I Quit Drinking*, and *List 10 Reasons Why You Drink*. I became inspired by people who had been where I was and were offering a hand with advice. I started asking myself questions like, *What did I like about drinking? What would I miss about it?* I began to quit while I drank, doubling down on my spiritual practices, building up my strength. I took cocktails to my Buddhist altar and drank and chanted and chanted and drank, so the *spirits* wouldn't become suspicious.

My last night of drinking was spent at a neighbor's going away gathering for her mother. I poured shots of tequila like a shooter gal at a Mexican restaurant for elderly people until I blacked out. I woke up remembering a lovely dream. I was a horse in a stall. The stall was opened by a young farmhand and I was released into a brilliant green pasture with tiny fragrant flowers. The farmhand was digging a hole in the distance when he suddenly stopped, wiped his brow and winked at me. As I lay in bed with the usual hangover, it was somehow different. I was resolved. Feeling whole, crisp and clear, I knew I was done with alcohol and drugs.

I had an older friend from the Bronx who told it like it is and gave me advice whether I asked for it or not. She had recently reprimanded me as I was leaving her downtown apartment, "Take care of yourself!" Her words rang in my ears and now I understood how to take her advice. As the saying goes, when you shut one door, another one always opens.

Soon after, another friend suggested some essential oils that had helped her tremendously. "Ok, send them," I said. When I touched the box, I had a moment. I knew what was inside would support me to move past alcohol. When I opened my first bottle of Joy, it brought me right back to that sunny pasture in my dream. Whereas alcohol and drugs lowered my frequency and left me hollow and jaded, the essential oils began purifying and enlivening my senses. They soothed and stabilized me, inspiring the courage that would keep me safe from addiction's claws.

Clairtangency - Clear Touching
A clairtangent person receives messages by touching or holding an object in their hands. They may pick up the vibration of the owner of the object.

4D

BLACKOUTS, SPIRITS AND THE SLAVE TRADE

"Whoso would be a man, must be a nonconformist. He who would gather immortal palms must not be hindered by the name of goodness, but must explore it if it be goodness. Nothing is at last sacred but the integrity of your own mind. Absolve you to yourself, and you shall have the suffrage of the world."

–Ralph Waldo Emerson

The word *alcohol* is derived from Arabic, al-kuhl which means *body eating spirit* and is the root origin of the English term, *ghoul* or *evil demon.*

Although I've not been sauced up for many years, I still avoid bars and gatherings with alcohol, not because I am tempted by the drink, but because I feel the negative entities. These low vibing discarnates and attachments hanging around remind me of when I would drink to excess and blackout. I now see that blacking out was my beautiful self leaving my body and being taken for a ride by low vibrational entities. That's why I couldn't remember whole periods of drinking episodes. My beautiful self would have to temporarily vacate my body to avoid poisoning. Then entities would literally take over my polluted body. My voice would sometimes change, I would ingest other harmful drugs, have low level sexual encounters and other kinds of self-destructive acts. The spirits (why do you think liquor is called spirits?) would hang around encouraging me to drink more, waiting to get a hold of me. This is part of what we call addiction in 3D reality.

A little background on alcohol.

Sugars in over ripe fruit attract microorganisms called yeast, which eat the fruit through a process called fermentation. Fermentation produces a chemical called ethanol, the type of alcohol in alcoholic beverages. Ethanol, like at the gas station, a toxic chemical which when consumed alone can cause coma and death.

Ancient cultures fermented drinks using the crops they had available in their regions. These drinks had relatively low percentages of alcohol because eventually the byproduct of fermentation kills off yeast. For thousands of years, the amount of alcohol one could consume was limited. How much mead can one drink at one sitting? How many bottles of wine? Then came the invention of distillation.

Ninth century Arabic writings talk about a process of boiling fermented liquids. Alcohol boils before water, so its vapors can be captured and cooled down. The result is distilled alcohol and is much more concentrated than any other fermented beverages. This concentrated form of alcohol was originally used primarily for medicinal purposes.

It then became an important component in Imperialism. When it was discovered that distilled spirits kill harmful microbes, alcohol became a staple on trade ships to preserve drinking water.

Cane sugar, harvested in European colonies in the Caribbean, was turned into rum. The Imperialists offered rum in trade with the Native Americans. They also brought brandy and gin to Africa in exchange for enslaved people. Spirits became a form of currency in these regions.

By the 1600's, alcohol was fueling global trade, i.e. the global thefting economy. Two of the consequences of this economy were the intricately connected slave trade and the blight of alcoholism. Cheers.

What happened last night? Oh. I may throw up. Sh*t. Where is my purse? Oh God, did I say that? I hope nobody remembers.

Alcohol is skirted around in health magazines and wellness circles. Are health practitioners afraid to face their own relationship to alcohol? Or do they fear losing clients by calling it what it is? Poison. Most guidelines recommend limiting alcohol consumption. It is so ingrained in our culture and people are so habituated, there's even a keg of beer reward at the end of marathons.

Look at how many gatherings and events revolve around it. Restaurants, weddings, galas, fundraisers, barbecues, pool parties, sandy beaches, date nights, meet-ups, etc., the bar is always center stage. Alcohol is synonymous with pleasure, relaxation, and having a good time in our culture.

Booze is a glamorized, romanticized, mass-produced, mass-marketed, dangerous, and addictive drug that is legal in much of the world.

"Now pour yourself a drink, put on some lipstick and pull yourself together."

–Elizabeth Taylor

Alcohol is the short end of the reward stick. It is an addictive substance that makes one progressively crave it more and more. It is also a depressant. As the brain tries to stay in balance under alcohol's depressive influence, the brain releases stimulants and stress hormones to counteract its effects. When one stops drinking, the brain is still racing to counteract the depressant factor and the overdrive of stimulants leaves one feeling nervous, anxious, tight and head-aching. All of these side effects are present while one is drinking, but the alcohol has anesthetized these feelings so you're not aware of them until the hangover.

Wow. Moving kind of slow this morning. Pang of guilt. Brain not working. Coffee. Whiff of shame? Nausea. Eggs? I know. A Bloody Mary.

Then as one drinks more alcohol, the symptoms mentioned above subside. The brain is seemingly working better because the feelings have once again been anesthetized and the negative thoughts temporarily soothed. The booze brain now believes that everyday problems, stresses and depression are relieved by drinking alcohol again. One doesn't see that drinking has caused these miserable symptoms in the first place. This is the cycle of alcohol dependency: the next drink relieves the anxiety and depression caused by the effects of the previous drinks.

Here is an exercise I did when I was ready to quit drinking.

List 10 Reasons Why You Drink

1. It's my reward after working hard all day.
2. It helps me shut off my thoughts.
3. It helps me control my eating disorder.
4. I enjoy drinking wine while I cook.
5. It helps me relax.
6. It helps me deal with my guilt.
7. It's socially acceptable.
8. It's my escape.
9. It slows me down.
10. It helps me sleep.

Now Your Turn, List 10 Reasons Why You Drink

1.
2.
3.
4.
5.
6.

7.
8.
9.
10.

THE CLAIRS

The stories in 3D were pages torn from my scrapbook of memories to illustrate examples of the clairsenses, or clairs, that we all possess. We all use our five physical senses to gather information and make decisions everyday. Our clairs, or superpowers, are how our intuition speaks to us. They give us information through impulses, signals, and clues. As we pay attention and tune into them, we begin to develop an individual language of communication with our clairs. By exercising them over and over, we learn to listen and read their signals, not to discount them but to rely on them.

The clairs are considered psychic abilities, unexplainable faculties which defy conventional science. They correspond with the five senses of seeing, hearing, touching, smelling, and tasting, as well as knowing and feeling. Although they are extrasensory perceptions, they're not at all extra and we all experience them! They are just not cultivated in our society because we would be too powerful and wouldn't want to get up and go work for *the man* anymore. Ha. Kidding. Not.

Most people have a few preferred or stronger

clairs that they use all the time. I paid the price earlier in my life by losing touch with my own and am so grateful I now allow them to guide me everyday.

Take a look at the clairs described below. Where do your natural abilities lie? Highlight any that feel strong for you.

Clairvoyance - Clear Seeing. You have vivid dreams, pictures in your mind, mini movies, visions. The stereotype is a fortune teller seeing the future in a crystal ball.

Clairaudience - Clear Hearing. You hear tones in your ears as confirmations. You hear birds confirming your thoughts. There is music in your dreams and you know that means there are important clues and messages for you. Maybe you hear voices, spirits talking to you. You have a natural ear for music. Musical prodigies are clairaudient.

Clairalience - Clear Smelling. Your nose knows. You smell things that others cannot. You can smell a rat, a dangerous situation and you can smell your way out of it. You pick up people's scents and know things about them. You may get a whiff of a relative's perfume or cigar after they have passed. You are sensitive to chemical fragrances designed to block your ability to use this sense properly.

Clairtangency - Clear Touching. Your hands are very sensitive, you may like to wear gloves. When you touch objects, you know more about them than just how they physically feel. This is the only clair that is not psychic information itself. The touch is a trigger that stimulates other clairs such as clairvoyance.

Clairgustance - Clear Tasting. You taste things in food that others do not. You remember tastes from dreams or when you think of a passed on loved one.

Clairsentience - Clear Sensing. You get information through sensing and feeling. You read other people's emotions or thoughts, which is also called telepathy. You may serve as a medium for people to connect with their passed on loved ones using sensory receptors and feelings.

Claircognizance - Clear Knowing. You trust your gut feeling. You get clear impressions, hunches and you follow them.

Instructions for developing and using clair gifts have been systematically removed from our textbooks and history. They are cataloged as fiction and explained as no more than fantasy, along with all magic. Our culture operates from a materialistic bias that denies the invisible. You are an oddball, on the fringe of society, if you do not spend your time in mainstream indoctrination, I mean, education. Education, jobs, householding, sporting events, and entertainment are all designed to help keep you busy and from exploring and spending time developing your clairs.

As you continue developing your clair gifts, you'll find yourself becoming an open conduit for divine work and will naturally begin to help others, while also attracting abundance into your life.

Signs you are already spending time in 5D:

- You fully accept yourself and others and are aware that judgment is just your mind trying to keep you safe. You let go instead.

- You know that your reality is created by your thoughts
  and you use your reality as a guide to clean up your thoughts.

- You walk forward in faith. You don't have to know the
  plan first.

- You start to eliminate toxic substances and people who do not support your growth.

- You are eating lighter as you develop your light, crystal
  line body versus the dense carbon body of 3D.

- You feel a oneness moving through your day,

connecting with nature, animals, people.

- You are giving more attention to your dream life and feeling the connection between waking and dreaming life.

- You are trusting your intuition more.

- You feel at ease, you do not feel rushed.

- You enjoy the process.

SLIPPING INTO NEW DIMENSIONS

I find our situation here on Earth very inspiring. It is a very exciting time and the reason I wrote this book is to help get the word out about how quickly we can transform our lives at this time. It's literally in the stars right now! We humans have potential beyond measure and the financial cartels who are sick with greed and fearful of us human beings know this. They spend a great deal of time and energy trying to stop us from waking up to our potential, from remembering, from coming out of our amnesia. Why? Because we are that powerful! Beings with something to hide can never really relax and play from a strong, clear place, no matter how many tricks they have up their sleeves. They are always on the defense. I find it fascinating, the more that is revealed about our ancient history, far beyond the flimsy narrative shown to us, the more excited I get! It is like a big puzzle of our birthright of superpowers coming together! I love puzzles!

Here's an illustration: centrally located in my quiet college town, there was a big bookstore where people gathered. One day it closed, replaced by a Starbucks. Now everyone goes to the big black hole of Starbucks. When I found out that Bill Gates was behind Starbucks, I was even more interested. Reading is being discouraged. Sugary drinks, full of toxic artificial chemicals and caffeine are being encouraged. Now people are also putting their money on a Starbucks card to pay for their drinks. You don't get interest on that card, why would you put your money there? So Starbucks is also a bank where they make money on your money and you pay with your cash and your health, seduced by a siren logo, like sailors led to their deaths by an enchanting song. Oh boy, my vibration is going down so fast with this line of thinking and I don't like it. I decide what I am going to do. Now that I have seen the playbook, I can make a choice. I am not going to get dragged down with negative thinking, I am going to read more books! I have the freedom to do that! I am lucky I can see the negative forces clearly and I make positive choices for my health and happiness accordingly.

Mother Earth is not just a planet, she is a consciousness and she is going through a historic shift in frequency, in vibration, and we humans are shifting with her. If you picked up this book you are sensing this. High Sobriety is about moving to higher levels of consciousness, higher dimensions and perspectives. We won't get to these new perspectives by falling for the same old tricks such as polluting ourselves with low-vibe substances such as booze, drugs, fast food, chemically laden household and personal care products, and Netflix. The jig is up. These old rackets being run on us, encouraging us to run them on ourselves, are wearing thin. We can refuse to be victims of our childhoods, our circumstances, or society's constructs. As victims we may gain attention and sympathy, but we lose our personal power.

It is such an exciting time to be human! Our DNA is being upgraded very quickly and shortcuts abound! Our lives can be turned around on a dime. As soon as I stopped drinking the *Kool Aid* and stepped out from the mass hypnosis, I soared to new heights.

Now, let's conspire together! Conspire comes from the Latin, *conspirare, to blend together, to harmonize.* Here is the definition that appears in the dictionary: *to make secret plans jointly to commit an unlawful or harmful act.*

"You keep using that word. I do not think it means what you think it means." - Inigo Montoya, The Princess Bride

Why is it unlawful or harmful to conspire, to act from opinions different from what is put out by the mainstream media? Going along with the herd is a subconscious survival mechanism to keep us safe. If we stick with the herd, we will live longer. But what kind of living? Surviving? Is it enough just to survive, when we can thrive once we cast off fear? What are we afraid of?

All fear can be distilled back to a fear of death. Are you afraid of what others think of you? Not being liked could cause ostracization from the herd, and there was a time when that meant death. We fear losing our livelihood, our home, and our resources. What would happen if we lost those things? We could starve, which is also a fear of death. Well, guess what? We are all going to die, so there is no point in fearing anything, especially when it is underhandedly instilled in us.

The intelligence agencies are well versed in psychological warfare. They take their marching orders from the small ruling class of dark occultists who have the secrets of the mystery schools and the ancient psychologists. They have studied human behavior and bullying tactics for a very long time.

They control the mainstream media and use repetitive mind control techniques which instill confusion, division and fear to those that follow. Yet when we awaken to see the man behind the curtain, when we study their history, and in addition become aware of our own behavior, they lose their power over us. Here's the good news – that's all they got! They are literally like The Wizard of Oz frantically maneuvering all the levers and dials to keep us looking at the big screen!

Governments do not have the manpower to contain us with armies, so using mind control techniques is an easy weapon they employ to keep us in a cycle of self-destructive behavior, while keeping us believing it is our right, our freedom to do so! An example from my life through song:

"You gotta fight for your right to party." - Beastie Boys

In the 80's the music business became corporate ruled and record companies no longer valued singer-songwriters or musicians. They started making artists fit into the corporate agenda. This is a song that my generation had pumped into our brains. It was written by The Beastie Boys, they meant it to be satire, yet it somehow became a twisted anthem of youth, a protest for my generation's right to deliberately destroy ourselves with drugs. I would hear this overpowering, obnoxious, stupid song and I would run as fast as I could away from it. It sent every jerkoff in the room into a frenzy and it was playing everywhere. We were poisoned with this "top selling single." Repetition is powerful.

Sit back a moment. Where did you get your preferences, your ideas of how things should be? Your likes and dislikes? Your values? Your moral compass? Are they really yours? Or could a lot of what you think of as your own thoughts been suggested to you repetitively? Why do we drink coffee? Alcohol? Were these ideas carefully orchestrated, countless times, through the media, school indoctrination, books, and Hollywood entrainment? I mean, entertainment. Could they have been slipped in so many times that you think they are your own preferences?

When I stopped drinking, I found that many of my ideas and motivations did come from Hollywood. As an old movie buff, a cinephile, I was absolutely spellbound. The Celtic Druids, ancient sorcerers, cast spells with magic wands made of holly wood. There are only vague legends about where the name Hollywood came from and holly trees are not native to Southern California. I was recently in a movie theater for the first time in about three years. I was invited by new friends and asked if it was a violent movie, they said it was a comedy, so I went. I was so bored that I decided to count how many times alcohol was visible in a shot. I counted 350 times before I got bored of counting. There were also a lot of shots in the film with people drinking coffee. Alcohol and coffee were the obvious repetitive content I saw with my naked eye. Then there are the product placements and the subliminal messages that are flashed so quickly on screen, only our subconscious mind sees them. Is it any wonder that as a cinephile I drank alcohol and coffee everyday? At one point, I even had a coffee maker set up in my bedroom so I wouldn't have to leave the room in the morning without a coffee jacking me up. Oh ya, I was hooked on caffeine as well.

The thing that bothered me about caffeine was not that it dehydrated me, cut off blood flow to my brain or made me a slave to the coffee pot. I learned that it shut down my conscious brain and made me more compliant. This rubbed the rebel in me the wrong way. I cut down to half-caffeinated, then to quarter-caffeinated, and I dealt with a horrible headache for a few days and I was free...

Once I eliminated the poisons from my diet and started cleansing them from my body, my self awareness sharpened. I started catching that some of my own beliefs were passed down from my parents' attitudes and further back from ancestors and even through shared DNA. I started to hear sayings and beliefs that were not mine, yet they would come out of my mouth. They started to stick out to me and I could now release them. I really enjoy identifying what I really like, what I really prefer, discovering who I really am.

Now, I do not use my parents and ancestors, or the forces controlling the media, as an excuse to play victim. I am simply pointing out these influences so I can spot them and be amused by their antics and their trembling fear of my power. They are terrified of me and anyone else who might state the obvious. *Hey look! The Emperor has got no clothes!* I prefer to go further into knowing myself, accepting myself, loving and caring for myself.

Brushing up on my clairs alters my perspectives and creates a reality of limitless freedom, joy, and connection in the fifth dimension. Most people only operate within the perspective of the third dimension, using their five senses to perceive things as three dimensional. *Past, Present, and Future.* But time does not really exist in a linear way, people just agree it does. We collectively have created something that is an illusion. We drag ourselves toward a future outcome in order to feel a certain way when we get there. When we manifest in the fifth dimension, when we allow ourselves to be in it, we collapse that heavy space, and experience eternal time in the quantum field. This is where everything exists electromagnetically as energy, as frequency, and the information field behind that. We can do anything there, create anything there as there is infinite time. The more time you spend in meditation on the present moment, the more you move to the fifth dimensional perspective.

SEEING in the Dimensions:

1st Dimension - You see only a point, one perspective.

2nd Dimension - You can see a flat surface, a line from 1st to 2nd dimension.

3rd Dimension - What most people can see, it's the physical realm, the human form, height, depth and width.

4th Dimension - A mind based perspective.

You can observe the body in 3D as well as some things you cannot see, including the mind and thoughts that trigger emotions.

5th Dimension - A *heart* based perspective.

From here you can see all of the other dimensions. By using your heart you can see the big picture. We are just going to look at the 3rd, 4th and 5th dimensions here as these are the dimensions we experience in this human form.

How one may HEAR the 3rd dimension:

I am trying.
I am wanting.
I am pursuing.
I will believe it when I see it.
Hard work pays off.
It's a dog eat dog world.
I am using resources which in turn contributes to climate change.
There's a right way and a wrong way.
There is not enough time in a day.
As I get older my body will decline.

This way of speaking runs very deeply in our culture, our families, our ancestors, past lives, and collective consciousness. We are encouraged to say these things, to tell it like it is. If we do not we are not being realistic or even lying.

How one may HEAR the 4th dimension:

I am getting ready to be ready.
I am healing from my childhood trauma.
I am working it out with my therapist.
The earth needs our help.
Let's talk about our issues.
I can reach my money goals.

How one may HEAR the 5th dimension using
Conscious Language:

I am the unlimited source of all.
All my needs are met in glorious ways.
I am safe to give freely as my heart guides.
All is right in the world.
I matter. I make a difference in the world.
I effortlessly attract the things I desire.
Everything always works out for me.
I am the creator of my reality.
My life is filled with love and purpose.
I am abundance, health, and wealth.
I am love, forgiveness, and acceptance.
I will see it when I believe It.
I am so grateful for my blessings.

Here is a chart of how we may FEEL in these dimensions:

3D	4D	5D
EGO PHASE	INTEGRATION PHASE	HIGHEST STATE
Pain/Suffering	Introspective	I Am Healed
Separate/Competitive	Integrating	I Am One
Struggling	Aligning	I Am Aligned
Linear	In a Gateway	I Am Nonlinear
Disconnected	Glimpsing	I Am Intuitive
Trapped	Immersed	I Am Effortless
Physical/Material	Lighter	I Am Divine Love

RAE LEONARD

5D

RAE LEONARD

FUN AND GAMES IN THE 5TH

The fun part has begun! Here are shortcuts, techniques, tips and tricks I use in my own life. When I discover a technique that interests me, I will practice it consistently for at least two months to form a new habit. Then I put it in rotation with other practices.

First Tip! Daily habits can be constricting. You may feel guilty if you miss a day. Whereas if you look at life in a cycle of a few days or a two week moon phase, you may find you bring in more good habits! I find 24 hours is too compact for all I want to do in a day. When I open up, loosen up my life into longer cycles, I feel more relaxed. I can miss a day. I can be gentle with myself and resume that good habit tomorrow, yet feel less stressed by linear time constraints.

THE 5D TREASURE HUNT

"I was looking in the open air and one of those glorious thistle things came down, I picked it up and brought it down and it looked like it was trying to get away. Just as if you caught an insect by one leg, like a daddy long legs. It seemed to be struggling to get away. Well I thought, it is not doing that, it is just the wind blowing. Then I thought again. Really? Only the wind blowing? Surely it is its structure in cooperation with the wind that enables it to move like an animal, using the wind's effort, not its own. It's a more intelligent being in a way because an insect uses effort, like a person who rows a boat. But the man who puts up a sail is using magic. He lets nature do it for him, with his intelligence to move the sail. That is the most highly skillful art of all. That is Taoism. It is perfection."

–Alan Watts

"We are here to fart around and don't let anyone tell you differently."

–Kurt Vonnegut

Who doesn't love a treasure hunt? How about running a treasure hunt anytime you want by just inviting your support team, your guides to come play with you? They are raring to go anytime, ready to give you clues, sometimes humorous ones! Clues to what? And what support team? Clues to find treasures in the 5th dimension, which will ultimately have you spending more and more time there and that's the point of the game! What your support team looks like is your personal preference. You might relate to them as spirit guides, ancestors of the land, animal guides, passed over loved ones, overdosed rock stars, ancient kings or queens, faeries, angels or religious figures. It's up to you.

Or how about this one? You can be on your own support team, living a parallel life where you have made different choices than the *you* in this 3D reality. There is a version of you, where you have gained different skills and experiences by traveling down other paths at crossroads you have come to. So there is no wrong path you have ever taken, because you have taken every path! So there is no place for regret in your life whatsoever. What a relief! Now the you, in all your parallel lives, is willing to share these lessons with you, in this 3D reality, instantly elevating you to 5D! I love bantering and learning from all the other versions of me on all the paths I have ever taken.

Whatever form your guides take, it doesn't matter as long as you feel in good company. You can engage them all day long or pick it up anytime you would like, your team is always there for you, ready to play.

There are many ways to start The 5D Treasure Hunt, it can be started from anywhere. It's easiest for me when I have a connection to Mother Nature. Maybe you like a sandy beach, a campfire, being on a boat, or in the garden. If you live in an apartment, open the window and look out.

I am an HSP (highly sensitive person), a hermitess, a wood nymph and I like a lot of alone time. I am sensitive to the elements. I don't like direct sun, salty water, strong wind. I like to enjoy nature, fresh air, birds, from a screened in porch or sitting on a mossy mound under a tree friend. Hiking is too stimulating for me. I need to be still, grounded and cozy to hear my guides.

I get all set up ready to play. I might start drumming or recite a mantra, knit, write in my journal, lie in my hammock, pull a tarot card. I just chill and wait for a clue, an affirmation from a bird guide, flying by and tweaking a confirmation of an idea that has just come to me and ... off I go.

Figure out what puts you in a receptive mood and works best for you.

An old friend pops into my head. Maybe I will give that person a call later. A mama cardinal flies by. O how pretty. She tweets. Ok Mama, I hear you. A leaf falls. My eyes follow it. Beautiful. More confirmation I will call my friend. I hear an airplane... Ok what else? A glimmer of sunlight peeps through the trees. I am open to more clues...I string clues together. I smear myself with oils, so I stay in 5D and I don't start analyzing anything. I allow guides to come in with quirky confirmations and I just keep open for clues. See how long you can stay engaged using your clairs. My two strongest clairs are claircognizance and clairalience. I just know things, I don't hear voices, things just come to me, especially through scent. What are your strongest clairs? Go back to The Clairs Chapter now, if you need a refresh on them.

Negative emotions are an invitation to play...

When I catch a negative thought or emotion. "Caught you you lil bugger. That is a judgment, I know because I feel stuck or maybe defeated or hopeless. Let me fix that." I pull myself back and engage my clairs. I widen my perspective visually using clairvoyance, as if I was widening a lens on a camera. This takes my focus off the negative emotion or thought I am experiencing in 3D. I go into a soft focus.

Now I engage clairaudience, I bring my attention to my Ajna chakra, my third eye. Awareness comes up and expands into my ears, I listen, I hear a ringing or frequency. I know I am in! All the sounds I hear are speaking to me. Chimes tingling, a branch falling, a car passing. I listen for sound or visual patterns occurring with my thoughts. Then I know that a thought which occurred when a dog barked is a message for me, a clue, an invitation to go further to find another clue. It is important to do this without any expectation or heaviness.

You can do this in a city park too. Use people's voices, words they say, the beeps of trucks backing up. Just listen for patterns, clues, sounds or sights corresponding to your thoughts. It's a practice. Keep blurring your vision, softening the lines of the 3D reality.

Remember, a 5D Treasure Hunt is a search for clues not answers. Have fun with your guides so they want to play with you more, give you more clues and eventually clear messages will come through. Don't spend time trying to figure out what the message is. Keep it light. One clue leads you to the next clue, while you are engaged and excited to play because the more you play, the more time you spend in a different perspective.

A synchronicity is another invitation to play The 5D Treasure Hunt. Carl Jung coined the term *synchronicity.* He called them chance occurrences from a statistical point of view, but that are meaningful in that they may validate paranormal ideas. Sometimes if I am all engaged or struggling in a 3D or 4D day, a synchronicity may get my attention. I hear a word on a podcast as I see that object in front of me, or I notice that some obscure word comes up twice in the same day, maybe I see it on a sign. Maybe someone brings up a city or topic that is new to me and then later it comes up again. Or I dream of something and there it is, in waking life. A song is speaking just to me. I pause and get in the game... "Ok Buddy Holly, I am listening. Tell me more..." I settle in with my clairs.

Go on treasure hunts often. You will get so good at it you will soon be able to soften your gaze, widen your peripheral vision and jump right into 5D! By playing the 5D Treasure Hunt, you strengthen your intuition and your connection to support that which cannot be seen in 3D, defying logic and rational explanation. You will have exchanges with them, dances with them, confirmations, private jokes and assistance. You can be on the path to treasure whenever you like and be lifted to a 5D reality where the harder lower dimensions do not hold you tight. Everything here is effortless, nothing to take too seriously and there is certainly nothing to stress about.

Best of all, when we are tapped into our intuition, deep in 5D, we understand that we are here in the 3D reality because it is simply a fun place for a treasure hunt.

WORDS ARE WANDS

"The difference between the right word and the almost right word is the difference between lightning and a lightning bug.

–Mark Twain

"The invisible forces are ever working for man who is always pulling the strings himself, though he does not know it. Owing to the vibratory power of words, whatever man voices, he begins to attract."

–Florence Scovel Shinn

Everything in the universe is made up of energy vibrating at different frequencies. Light, sound, heat, motion, even scent are all forms of energy that are vibrating. Even things that look solid are made up of vibrational energy fields at the quantum level, including every single cell of our human body. Words are an easy way to affect vibration or in other words ...

everything!

Prophesies.

Imagine little ol' you making prophecies. Well, you already do all day long with the words you speak. A prophecy is like the more commonly used term, affirmation. I use the word prophecy because when you affirm, to me it sounds a bit unsure. When you prophesize, you have no doubt of your announcement, you are making an inspired declaration of divine will and purpose.

The Power of I AM.

Using I AM, instantly activates Source Energy. When you invoke these powerhouse words you initiate them into the physical plane. They were given to Moses by God when he asked the question, "Who shall I say sent me with this message?" The answer given was, I AM THAT I AM. Everything is the I AM. It is The vibration and the image of you, the image of God, the image of the universe. You instantly become whatever you say when you use I AM. You step into the Power of Beingness. You are announcing what you are to the universe and the universe instantly responds, echoing back.

Be aware of what you are stepping into. I AM tired, I AM sad. Better is, I AM feeling tired at the moment. Feelings are fine and feelings change. Float in and float out of tiredness, don't step in with your whole identity. Skip the contraction, I'm. It bypasses the resonant power of I AM. Open your mouth, open your throat, and step into the beingness of I AM.

Minimize the use of the following words and phrases:

WANT.

We are human *beings* not human *wanters.* Wanting is needy, powerless and whiny. Wanting is not the state you choose to be in. When you say, "I want a new job" the universe reflects back, "They want a new job. They want a new job." Endlessly you are wanting. Instead of saying, "I want a new job" or "I want my soulmate." Be the exciting creator of your dream career or soulmate, by switching that sentence up for, "I am so excited about my new career!" The universe reflects back, "They are so excited about their new career!" You've stepped in and the universe must deliver. It is a law

People expect us to talk about the negative things happening in our lives, to downplay ourselves, it's a cultural norm. Even if you are healthy, wealthy, wise and free, it sounds boastful to say so. *Stay down lil' doggies. Don't get too big for your britches.* We are trained to word much of who we are in a negative light.
"Oh you just got a new job?"
"Ya, but, it only has 2 weeks paid vacation a year."
"Oh, you started your own business?"
"Ya but, I have to pay my own health insurance."

BUT.

All day long people say something positive, they uplift their frequency, their vibration, then clamp it right down with the word *but.* "I acquired a camper van, I love the freedom it brings me, *but* the gas is so pricey to travel with it."

When you use the word *but*, you negate all the aspects of what you have said before. So in this example, all the freedom of the van, all the positive vibes, POOF. Gone. You just negated them. Listen to people say the word but in their sentences. It is always a downward vibration. Use the word *yet* instead, you are just comparing, giving more information. You can talk about the pros and cons of something without dampening the positive aspects. Get in the habit of using *yet* instead of but. "I just got a Condo on the beach! It's great! *Yet* I have to rent it out for a few years to make some payments on it."

SHOULD

Should is a big heavy word, laden with obligation, guilt and criticism. *Should* is best replaced with *could* or *I would like to*, or *I would enjoy*.

"I *should* take the garbage out." How does that feel? Like putting on the hair shirt? Judgment? Self criticism? How about, "I think I would enjoy taking the garbage out, I'll get some fresh air!" And when talking to others, even if they ask for advice, let them know what they *could* do as opposed to what they *should* do. The energy is so different! It's so much more uplifting.

I DON'T KNOW.

We all hear this all day long, talk about repetitive content. We are a culture of not knowing. Let's transform to a people of knowing! People Of Knowing, Unite!

Replace *I don't know* with *I choose to know*. When

you use, *I don't know,* the universe echoes back, *They don't know.* You will be moving forward not knowing. When you say, *I chose to know,* the universe responds to your command! *They chose to know,* bring that person answers now! Hop to it!

In the past, before I became aware of Conscious Language, when I made a mistake or just didn't yet understand the process of how to do something, these words came out before I even knew it. I'm an idiot. Cancel cancel, delete, delete on that!!

Now when this phrase arises in my thoughts, I switch it up as it starts to come out of my mouth, *I AM the most brilliant loving being, made in God's image, who is fascinated and learning all the time.*

Make your own prophecies and repeat them in the mirror daily. Use only positive words. Here is one of mine:

I AM a cosmic conscious creator and I AM holding my attention on all that is well. I allow the conceptions that I conceive. I clear any old creations that no longer serve me. I Am the power and presence of the Goddess and I experience everything that I prefer moving along on super highways through neural pathways, created with this invocation.

Make it personal for you, something that you like to repeat that rolls off your tongue and makes you feel so good! Repeat it as many times as you need to to get that empowered feeling going.

HOW TO SHARE THE POWER OF I AM

I was educated at *The School Of Cool* in NYC. Before I understood the power of words and used them as magic wands, people would ask me, "How are you? What are you up to?" I had catchy cool responses for when people tried to get too close. "Oh you know, boozin .... brawlin." Or my other favorite, "The usual, classically underachieving." I energetically pushed any meaningful connection with the person away. I established a safe force field around myself and the person would back off with a chuckle.

Now that I do not need to put up a guard, I love to take the opportunity to connect with people and uplift with them. I turn the conversation around by saying, "Flipping fabulous! How about you? What are you excited about?" If they respond with something like "Well I'm just tired."I guide the conversation. "So you are excited to get some rest?"
"Yes, I'm excited to get some rest."
"Wonderful!" I keep, nodding my head enthusiastically. They usually say it again. "Ya, I am excited to get some rest."

People love to talk about themselves and this gives them the opportunity to do that as they use the power of I AM. They just feel better. Try this, you will be uplifting everyone's energy and will notice they always perk up and are happy to see you!

CANCEL CANCEL DELETE DELETE

An easy correction you can have fun with is when you catch yourself, using an I AM in a way that doesn't serve you best.

"I AM so tired." Ooops, caught that. "Cancel cancel delete delete. I AM so looking forward to my vacation!" That's it, so simple, just catch your less than perfect prophecy and cancel cancel delete delete. Done.

PIVOTING WITH RELIEF STATEMENTS

When you find yourself going down a rabbit hole emotionally, say you see something on sale that you just purchased retail. Your perception is you made a mistake. You should have waited...bummer. Now you notice your perception is not bringing you joy. Pivot! You try on a better feeling thought, such as 'Oh well, money is a renewable resource.' or "I Am happy I supported that business and someone made a full commission on that purchase." Whatever statement brings you some relief from the negative emotion you were feeling. Pivot and find a better feeling statement.

MANTRA

A mystical formula of invocation many times originating from the Sanskrit language and an easy way to harness vibration. The Sanskrit language has a unique resonance because it has more soft sounds then hard sounds in it and soft sounds are more resonant.

Om is the Origin Seed Mantra, from which all other sounds and words come.
Linguistically, Om, AH...UU..MM incorporates all sounds that can emanate from the human throat. The sound created by chanting Om, vibrates at the frequency of 432Hz, which is the same vibrational

frequency as the earth's natural electromagnetic pulse, the same as everything in nature, the frequency of the universe itself. So by chanting Om, we symbolically and physically tune into that same frequency and connect with all other beings and forces. The words themselves carry powerful mystic meanings. Yet you don't need to understand what the words mean to benefit from chanting mantras. You can just tap in! I like to add a mantra to the beginning of my five minute meditation and also after yoga asana. You chant in the car or with a group, called kirtan, or chant along with a kirtan artist. Find chants that feel good to you! When you recite a Sanskrit mantra you are spending time in 5D.

My List of Greatest Hit Mantras:

OM - chill, connect

NAM MYOHO RENGE KYO - Get it going on

WAHE GURU WAHE JIO - Get high on the breath

The entire George Harrison album Chant and Be Happy! - on repeat

FOOD. GOOD.

"One should enjoy food and have fun. It's one of the simplest and nicest pleasures."

–Julia Child

"It can't be what you eat, as we all know those skinny women who eat whatever they want."

–Abraham

"Food. Good."

–Frankenstein

I know I am far from alone on my long and winding food trip. We live in this food obsessed culture with food at our fingertips at all times, 24 hour grocery stores, modern refrigeration, all night diners, food on social media. Yet there are many people on this planet who are hungry.

We have nurturing memories of loved ones pushing food at us as a way of showing love, comfort and affection. We were praised for cleaning our plate. If you are reading this book you probably have access to food and food to excess. Yet most of us are only a few generations from experiencing food shortages, war, famine, The Great Depression. True hunger is a threat we have all experienced through our ancestral bloodlines embedded in our DNA, the collective consciousness and past lives. Our feelings and ideas have not caught up with our new reality of overabundance of food. Also, the quality of our soil and the food it produces has dramatically degenerated over the past fifty years, so most of this over abundance is not nutrient rich. We are eating more, nourishing our bodies less. No wonder it's so challenging to keep our relationship to food in balance.

The Standard American Diet (SAD) benefits Big Agra and Big Pharma, with no mention of things that have really helped me, so I thought I'll mention them! Enzymes, fermented foods, superfoods, supplements, food combining, cleansing the body, the digestive/elimination cycles of the body and the timing of eating, have all improved my health as well as assisted in my transformation! Let's look at some attitudes and practices around eating first.

Gratitude for our food! When we pause and express gratitude for the food in front of us we keep connected to it, yet we do not have to feel pressured to eat it, as that undermines our innate sense of discernment, of being satisfied. Whether we say a prayer or just pause and give thanks it makes a difference.

Chew, chew, chew. Digestion starts in the mouth. I didn't really catch on to this until I heard chew, chew,

chew and mix your saliva around with your food! Oh that's fun! It's like getting to play with your food and you really taste it more as well as liquefying it!

Go for satisfaction, not fullness. Many people say, "I am full" when they are done eating. But who wants to be full of food? How about, "I feel satisfied." Then sit back and enjoy that feeling.

There is no waste! Don't waste food is a message many of us received. The entire concept of waste is false. The subject of waste in general is a major bummer, a valve closer, a blocker of the flow of our energy and it is the opposite of what we really are. We are limitless beings with a stream of never ending resources flowing through us. There is no waste. It's the falsehood of not enoughness and as creators of our own reality, we have created a lot of food. Eating food we do not have an appetite for, can never be good for us. Even if it is the most vital, high vibrational food on earth, overloading our digestive system will not replenish us and will not feed a hungry person elsewhere.

Offer food back to earth! Compost! Giving food to the worms, insects and microbes feels alot better than scraping it into a plastic garbage bag. We make rich earth by composting and keeping our connection to the cycle of food.

Time to eat! The Industrial Revolution influenced the times that we eat. 7am is breakfast, not necessarily because you feel an appetite, but because you go to work and won't be able to eat until an assigned time later. 12 noon is a break for lunch and 6pm dinner on the table, so you go to bed early and get up and do it again. These hours are guided by profit for maximizing assembly line work, not for listening to our bodies for appetite cues. We are designed to go periods of time without food. Our ancestors did not have stoves attached to their bodies preparing 3 square meals a day.

As a child I was looking for pleasurable food experiences in all the wrong places, such as a typical day attending public school in the US. Yikes. Did you ever notice how public school cafeterias resemble prison cafeterias? I never liked getting up at an assigned time. I did it because there was a breakfast reward, a short sugary rush, cold cereal with cow's milk. School was 40 minute segments designed not to go much in depth on any subject, cutting short my curiosity and free form thinking, I just made it to lunch. Possibly there would be some pleasurable experience after being locked up and herded around all morning. Although I had no real appetite, it was already short circuited by gobbling cold sugar mash at 7 am. I had no time to let my body's natural elimination cycle kick in. Who cares, let's stuff more food in. I qualified for the free hot lunch program. Although I didn't care for my name being announced over the intercom. It sounded like, "Will the poor little fat girl come down to the office to pick up your lunch tickets?" My cheeks burned with free hot lunch humiliation. Tacos, pizza, tater tots, were a break from the monotony of the school day, as well as a distraction from pain. Any pleasure was soon replaced by all my energy being concentrated on my overstuffed stomach. Depression set in as I dragged myself through the rest of the school day. As soon as I was just not stuffed, the clock said it was time for the next potential food reward, dinner. It was usually some nutrient wasteland like boxed mac and cheese. I was constantly clogged and dazed, never putting together the connection between low vibrational food and my depleted physical and emotional state. I was just on a daily, not so merry go round, searching for food that made me feel good. I was an addict.

Notice how different food and the time that you eat it, makes you feel! At some point, I realized I did feel somewhat better if I didn't eat food that I didn't love. Yet sometimes I would lose control of my emotions, gorge on a tub of ice cream or a bag of chips and resort to the ever popular teenage girl stand by, binging and purging. Stuffing myself, stuffing my emotions, until I felt something ... there it is ... self loathing. Then I was into the bathroom to stick my finger down my throat. I wished I had the discipline of the anorexics. They never let temptation pass their lips. Unlike me, who was clumsy, lethargic, constipated and out of control.

When I got older and walked around the city, I discovered foods with a higher vibration, health food joints with organic fruits and vegetables where I could grab a smoothie, Middle Eastern and Mediterranean places with lots of vegetarian options. I found I was a grazer, I felt much better with fruit and nuts and seeds to keep me feeling energized and upbeat, and then one substantial meal a day. I liked eating around 4 or 5 when I could then really enjoy it and rest and digest. It takes a lot of energy to process a meal and having a breakfast or lunch weighed me down where depression could easily get a grip. Grazing on high vibrational, live foods, full of enzymes keeps me upbeat, moving through my day.

I am Hungry. A statement full of lack and victimization as if you are experiencing true hunger and going to die. Most of us have never known real hunger in this incarnation, speaking it puts you into a desperate state. No thanks! We don't want to play any *Hunger Games.* It is a dramatically misused word that causes anxiety when we could just be feeling excitement. "Wow! I am feeling appetite. I am so lucky to be feeling appetite because it means I am looking forward to eating soon! I can't wait to prepare a lovely meal. It is coming and I will enjoy it so much!" Experience the joy of appetite.

Never eat when you are not feeling an appetite. No matter how rude it seems or how good the food looks. Don't eat by the clock or because you are bored or stressed or it will make others feel more comfortable. Wait until you are signaled by your body that you are ready for food. Cherish your health above the temptation of food! I get excited when I feel an appetite because I love to eat and now my body is telling me it is also ready!

WAY OF THE LEMON

Hey! Guess what? Jubilant health and wellness is your birthright! All dis-ease is waste accumulation turned toxic in your body. It is stuck stuff, stale thoughts, unprocessed emotions.

When I quit drinking alcohol I had many shifts in my perceptions. I was excited about discovering more natural highs. At first the shifts in perceptions were subtle. Yet I sensed that positive side effects were going to compound and they did. I still suffered from chronic constipation and urinary tract infections. I was always wanting to eat, yet never knowing where I was going to put my next meal .. a super unsatisfying state. I knew I needed to lose waste. One reason I had started drinking more wine was so I wouldn't just keep filling my belly up with more food that wasn't going anywhere. Ya, a great health solution, booze.

I had always been interested in the Master Cleanse. I saw disciplined yogis benefiting from the physical and spiritual aspects of a cleansing practice. I sensed my deep rooted feelings of unworthiness and shame were stuck in my body and it didn't matter whether this old gook was coming from this life, a past life or the collective consciousness, I was ready to let go.

I was ready to allow my own healing. I used my mantra. I AM the one who lets everything go and I AM the one who lets everything come.

I set my mind to it, which is hardest part. I found a support group and started The Ten Day Complete Master Cleanse Program with Tom Wolloshyn. His program is descended from the original Master Cleanse Protocol created by Stanley Burroughs in the 1940's. This program is about taking responsibility for your health into your own hands and uses other tools including Louise Hay's book *Heal Your Body.*

This was the best decision I have ever made for my health, my intuition, my connection to nature, my practice of deep listening. It was like I cleaned out my cell receptors, antennas, my aura as well as losing pounds of waste I no longer needed trapped in my body.

I went on the ten day cleanse, ten times a year for two years. It was so beneficial that it has become part of my lifestyle. I now look forward to quarterly cleanses and all the gifts it brings!

Most of us have a lot of waste in our colon, because even if we have one elimination for every meal we eat a day, we still leave behind approximately a tablespoon of waste. So if you eat three meals a day over 50 years, that's 54,750 tablespoons left behind. This leftover waste turns to layers and layers of hardened plaque held in place partly with the emotions we were feeling at the time of eating the food. Tough stuff, rubber tire tough. But there is good news!

Our bodies come with our own built-in cleaning/detoxifying/healing cycle, just like dishwashers! This cycle is designed to kick in when we take a break from the usual digestion cycle of constantly processing solid food. When we consume this liquid diet and allow the natural healing mode of our bodies a chance to turn on, they are capable of miraculous things.

FREQUENTLY ASKED QUESTIONS:

What is the difference between a fast and a cleanse?

When you fast, you take in no nutrition forces. On The Ten Day Master Cleanse you take in calories to keep up your metabolic rate high so you are not hungry. Most of the time you have great energy, your body gets the nutrition it needs while not spending time digesting food which takes a lot of energy.

Will I be hungry? Weak?

No, when you are hungry you drink another lemonade which provides perfect nourishment. Sometimes you may feel toxins being released from your system like old stuck emotions and waste. Lie down, give your body extra rest, run a healy program, use some Young Living Essential Oils, trust the process. There is more on both in later chapters.

What is the difference between a juice cleanse and The Ten Day Master Cleanse?

Juice cleanses are beneficial. Yet you do not eliminate layer after layer of old rehydrated plaque and waste from your colon. You also may not deal with the emotional component of cleansing at all.

I have a friend who got sick on the master cleanse, will I get sick?

I have done many cleanses with many people

and people experience many ways of healing, it is a varied and personal experience. Some people have heavy emotions come up or do not have a good support team in place or maybe they don't follow the directions. Usually any unwell feelings can be moved through by resting and drinking more lemonade.

Can I just do colonics?

I had done many colonics before I found master cleansing. I like this comparison. Say you had a factory and in it there is an important machine for running your factory efficiently. This machine runs on solid fuel. It separates the useful fuel from the solid waste by-product. This machine runs many times a day, everyday. You hire a service to do machine maintenance. They give you two options.

Option 1: They shut the machine for a few hours and run a hose through the out end where the solid by product usually comes out. They flow water up a bit up into the machine. It does not run all the way through the machine and spills back out the same way it went in, clearing out waste that is fairly loose. When they are done the machine is turned on again as you need to get it back up and running to process the fuel again for your factory.

Option 2: The maintenance service runs a liquid fuel all the way through the machine for ten days. This liquid will soak, rehydrate, loosen and eliminate hardened waste, over and over again. They continue to pour in the liquid and vibrate the inside of the machine to loosen and peel away layer after layer of waste. The machine also gets a full tune up and other upgrades. You also don't need to shut down the machine, it will run on this liquid fuel as it cleans the essential parts.

Which do you think sounds more effective?

What is the difference between a master cleanse and The Ten Day Master Cleanse?

The alliance of the ingredients in the master cleanse are very powerful, yet most regular master cleanse protocols do not include any herbal laxatives and without solid food as a catalyst for peristalsis, you will not eliminate the waste you have loosened. This is a big part of why so many people say "Oh I tried the master cleanse, it didn't work for me." Imagine deep cleaning your house and not taking out the garbage? Often master cleanse protocols do not include intentions and declarations and are often used as a diet not as a way to let go of waste and belief systems.

Can I do less than a ten day cleanse? That's all the time I have.

It is a ten day program. In my experience you don't even have all the food out of your system for three or more days. You need time on the cleanse for your body to go into healing/detox mode and stay in it, for maximum benefit. Think of how long you have been accumulating old stuff in your body. It is a ten day program, do longer if you like, not shorter. The commitment is harder than the cleanse itself. Set an intention, a health goal for the cleanse, trust and have faith you can do it. Make yourself the priority for 10 days. You are worth it!

I AM Statements and Prophecies Turn The Tide

You can use any of these or write your own. Say them in a mirror daily until you mean it!

I am doing this cleanse to reset my health and reset my mind.

I am doing this cleanse to let go of old stuck beliefs that are no longer serving me.

I release the past and live in the present moment.

I release the things that no longer serve me.

I trust the process of life.

You can also examine the pay off you currently get for staying in your dis ease, ie. being a victim of your ill health, not trusting change or maybe staying in the familiar safe pattern. This is the real challenge of The Ten Day Master Cleanse, more so than simply the program of hydrating, dissolving, loosening and eliminating waste in your body (which is so effective and satisfying).

The Ten Day Master Cleanse is a tool of transformation, a tool for divine connection and a tool for lightness as you exchange density, a thick feeling, for a crystalline, sparkling clear nature.

INGREDIENTS

LEMONS: The unsung super food! Lemons are unique in that they are an acid food yet highly alkalizing. They are a natural cleansing agent, breaking down mucus and calcifications in the body and have many minerals, including magnesium, potassium, phosphorus, sodium, zinc copper, selenium and iron. Lemons cleanse the blood, flush bacteria from the urinary tract, helps loosen toxins from deep tissues and organs as they tone them with their astringent character. Lemons make things sparkle! Think about what happens when you rub greasy hands with lemon juice.

MAPLE SYRUP: Maple Syrup provides one with the fuel during your cleanse. Think of sap as a tree's blood. Sap is the sugar produced in a tree's leaves by the process of photosynthesis, mixed with water brought up through the tree's roots. The sugar in sap provides the fuel for the tree to grow and thrive. It is not processed like cane sugar and has many nutrients and vitamins.

CAYENNE PEPPER: Full of antioxidants, good for digestion and the capsaicin in cayenne can protect the body from inflammation. Cayenne pepper may lower blood pressure and keep blood vessels healthy.

WATER: Nature's strongest solvent. It carries nutrients and oxygen to your cells, flushes bacteria from your bladder, aids digestion, improves brain function, cushions joints and protects organs and tissues.

THE TEN DAY MASTER CLEANSE SUPPLY LIST

- 40 to 45 organic lemons
- 1 gallon of maple syrup
- Organic cayenne pepper
- A juicer (not metal)
- 24 oz mason jar
- Young Living thieves oil 15 ml
- Young Living oregano oil 15 ml
- Young Living thyme oil 15 ml
- Young Living digize blend 15 ml
- Young Living tummywise roll on
- Young Living vitality oils such as tangerine,

lime, cinnamon
- Vegetable capsules size 0
- Young Living detoxzyme or essentialzymes
- Swiss Kriss herbal laxatives
- Sea salt
- Herbal teas (optional)

TRANSITION DAY SUPPLY LIST

- Organic oranges
- Other organic fruits
- Organic vegetables / vegetable broth

PREPARATION DAY

Eliminate the following:
- Caffeine
- Alcohol
- Meat
- Dairy
- Sugar

CLEANSE DAY ONE

STEP 1

Upon arising take two Swiss Kriss herbal laxatives. Start with two, if you need more you can up the dosage slowly, 2 ½ etc. I keep some by my bed, I take them with some water before I get up.

OR Prepare a salt flush. Dissolve 2 tsp, not tbsp, sea salt in 32 oz hot/warm water. Sit for ten minutes to sip/drink it. Not too fast, it could come up. Not too slow, it wont work. Be ready to be near a bathroom for the next 1 ½. After that you should be fine to go about your day.

STEP 2

Prepare your lemonade using the recipe below. It can be warm or cool but not too hot. If it burns your finger it is too hot. You don't want to destroy the live enzymes.

LEMONADE RECIPE

- Juice of one lemon
- 4 tablespoons maple syrup
- Pinch cayenne pepper
- 16 oz pure water
- 24 oz mason jar

You can keep a few days of lemons in your fruit bowl on the counter, refrigerate the rest. Roll your room temperature lemon to get the juices flowing. Juice your lemon. You can juice by hand or use an electric juicer, just not a metal juicer as metal reacts with citrus. I use an old fashioned enamel covered citrus press. Pour into a 24 oz jar. Add the maple syrup, a pinch of cayenne pepper and 16 oz pure water. You can add a drop of vitality oils such as lime or cinnamon for variety. Stir. Drink immediately.

STEP 3

Make up your parasite busting capsules. The cleanse is a great time to get rid of them! They are already weakened and hangry. Hit them when they are down!

Prepare a dropper bottle (4 oz is good but whatever size you have works) with ⅓ rd each of thieves, oregano and thyme. Pop off the plastic aperture on the oil bottle and use a dropper to fill the dropper bottle with ⅓ rd of each oil. Shake before use. With this prepped dropper bottle, put 9 drops in three capsules and take them three times a day. You can make up a bunch of capsules ahead of time and stick them in the freezer for convenience. Do not prepare extra capsules and leave them out, the oils will melt the veggie capsules.

STEP 4

Take six to nine digestive enzymes during the day. Detoxyme or Essentialzymes.

STEP 5

Put out a tray with your supplies on it so you are always ready to make lemonade. Stand right there in the kitchen and drink your lemonade down right away. FOCUS. Make your lemonade fresh, open your throat and drink it. Opa! Attack your lemonade and you will instantly feel energized and balanced. Don't vacillate. The live enzymes in lemons degrade every minute they are exposed to oxygen and light. Whenever you feel the least bit of appetite, make another lemonade. Have as many as you would like, no limit. At least four mason jars a day. Later in the evening take three more oil capsules.

Before bed take two or more Swiss Kriss tablets, however many you need to be eliminating at least three or more times a day.

CLEANSE DAYS TWO THROUGH TEN

Same as Day One! You can drink herbal tea and water to change it up but not too much, you don't want to fill up on tea or water and not get the energy and nutrients you need. You can also munch on some lemon rinds as a snack. You're getting plenty of water with your lemonade so you don't really need to drink extra water, yet you can. If you feel anything but incredibly vital and sparkly, drink more lemonade and no short cuts, make it fresh! Do not prep a large jug of lemonade ahead of time for convenience sake. This is your food for the next ten days. No skimping on your sustenance.

Make the space in your life. Take a few vacation days to start your cleanse off smoothly. If you are the cook for your household, tell your loved ones you are taking steps for your health, not just trying a fad diet. Tell them you would love their understanding and support. Order take out for them to start your cleanse so you are not preparing meals, yet they are taken care of. Schedule your cleanse when you have a fairly open schedule.

If you have appointments or work outside the home, you may make a lemonade concentrate to take with you. A concentrate is an acceptable option ONLY when making a fresh juice is not an option. The maple syrup preserves the lemon juice a bit, but adding water to the concentrate will destroy its integrity quickly. Water is a solvent.

LEMONADE CONCENTRATE RECIPE

Juice of two lemons
Eight tbsp of maple syrup
Mix together in a mason jar

Pack a tote with:
Empty 24 oz mason jar
Mason jar with lemonade concentrate
Small container with cayenne
Pure water if none will be available

Mix 4 tbls. of the concentrate to 20 oz of water. Add a pinch or two of cayenne.
Do not add your cayenne to your jar of concentrate. The cayenne will become too spicy!

SWISS KRISS OR SALT FLUSH? This is the question...

Swiss Kriss - Easy to take, very effective, unpredictable.
Salt Flush - Not as easy to take, effective, more predictable

I do not take Swiss Kriss on the mornings that I have errands or work outside of the house. I don't want to be in a panic finding a restroom! If I am going to be out of the house for many hours, I do a salt flush, at least two hours before I leave. A salt flush will move through the system in an hour and a half, giving you flexibility for the rest of the day. Then you don't have to think about elimination the rest of the day. The important thing is that you are doing something every day and night on the cleanse to keep the flow of waste going out of your body.

Feeling low energy, odd or having an occasional headache is normal, you are detoxing. The toxins plus old emotional baggage are the waste that has to come up and out. Sometimes when we are cleaning, things seem messier. Don't judge the cleanse until you have completed the ten day program. Drink more lemonade and take a nap. Listen to your body. It speaks to you.

TRANSITION DAY

1. Juice your oranges and enjoy fresh squeezed orange juice. Not too fast!
2. You can also eat some oranges.
3. Prepare your vegetable soup.

Enjoy the best soup you have ever made... until your next cleanse!

VEGETABLE SOUP RECIPE

Ingredients:
Any vegetables you like, such as, onions, garlic, potatoes, cabbage, carrots, beets, peas, kale, collards, vegetable stock, your own or *Better Than Bouillon*, fresh herbs, thyme, rosemary, sage, oregano, good sea salt, Malden or pink himalayan.

Dice a large onion and caramelize it by adding it to a stock pot with avocado oil on the lowest heat possible for 30 minutes, stirring often with a pinch of sea salt and fresh herbs. Add other veggies and fill pot with stock until you have the ratio of water to veggies you like.

MY AFTER CLEANSE DIET AND LIFESTYLE

"The serpent is in man, it is the intestines. The belly is a heavy burden: it disturbs the equilibrium between the soul and the body; it fills history. It is responsible for all crimes. It is the mother of vices. The colon is king." -Victor Hugo

My eating regime is a result of lifelong trial and error and deep listening to my body. It works for me. I eat about 50% to 60% raw foods, fruits, vegetables, nuts, seeds, and lots of fermented foods like sauerkraut, kimchi, kombucha. I don't like eating animals because it is not kind and desensitizes me. I ask myself, would I eat this food if it was raw? If the answer is no, I eat it sparingly.

I was on a liquid mono diet for over 200 days spanning two years and I now cleanse about four times a year. I discovered that my body works really well on a fairly liquid diet as I was severely constipated most of my life. I am now aware that everything I put in my mouth must be broken down and what is not needed should come out quickly. I am connected to the process now. Digestion starts in the mouth and I chew my food, mixing it with salvia to a liquid form. I like it to have a smooth ride on a complicated route. Now I am blessed to have my body working perfectly and my weight no longer thought at all, as the five to ten pounds I had always struggled to keep off were actually accumulated waste in my gut.

THE BODIES NATURAL DIGESTIVE CYCLE

4am-noon is the body's elimination time. When I wake up, I drink at least 42 oz of hot water with lemon. There is an upcoming chapter on the benefits of hot water. I also take my supplements at this time as it's a good time for me to remember. I flush my system and then take my supplements around noon.

Noon-8pm is the body's eating and digestion time. I snack on fruit then add seeds and nuts, mostly fruit and smoothies. I categorize food into sweet and savory. I have found for me personally that if I eat sweet things I easily stop. When I eat savory foods I feel less control. I basically stick to raw fruits during the day and then eat one savory main meal a day around 4 pm.

I steam vegetables in a soft steamer, *The Vitaliseur de Marion*. This pot, which does not heat food above 100 degrees is a gem and is not comparable to any other steamers. It is designed with exact proportions between the tank, the sieve and the lid, as well as the diameter of the holes and the diameter of the Vitaliseur which optimizes cooking performance. These parameters really make the difference! Vegetables steam quickly and retain their vitamins and enzymes, the taste and the colors of the food are incomparable! I load it with squash, potatoes, carrots, turnips, kale and collards. I add kimchi, drizzle butter or tahini, sea salt and some crunchy chili oil. It is so simple and so satisfying. I love my Vita! I also like to have a little dessert, a few squares of chocolate or something and then I am done.

8pm-4am is your body's absorption and assimilation time. Good thing because I am sleeping.

MY DAILY SUPPLEMENT LIST

Ningxia Red - The Ningxia Region in China is bursting with Centenarians where they consume *the red diamonds*. These are wolfberries or goji berries, one of the most nutrient dense foods on the planet. Super high in antioxidants, vitamins and minerals, Ningxia Red is an ally of anti-aging and disease, supports eye health, energizes the body and supports normal cellular function. I drink it everyday.

Sulfurzyme powder- Healthier hair, smoother skin, stronger nails, yes please! MSM helps your cells stay supple!

ICP Daily - a yummy prebiotic and fiber drink. It contains powerful ingredients including agave inulin, prickly pear cactus extract and an essential oil blend of fennel, anise, tarragon, ginger, lemongrass and rosemary essential oils. These ingredients support cardiovascular and immune system health. They maintain a healthy gut microbiome and aid in the body's natural detoxification process.

AminoWise - This is if you get in a hard workout or want extra amino acids for your circulatory system. I love the taste and I use it to get extra minerals in my body as well as another glass of hot water.

Mindwise - Wakes up my brain. It supports cardiovascular and cognitive health. With a vegetarian oil cold pressed from sacha inchi seeds harvested from the Peruvian Amazon, it has a high proportion of unsaturated fatty acids and omega-3 fatty acids.

Multigreens Capsules - gets me my green stuff! They are rich in antioxidants to support healthy cell function. They also support memory, mood and other nervous system functions, made with spirulina, alfalfa sprouts, barley grass, bee pollen, eleuthero, Pacific kelp and essential oils!

Agilease - I woke up on my 50th birthday and I creaked. Two weeks on Agilease and I was back to jumping out of bed. It helps promote joint and cartilage health, mobility and flexibility through reduction of inflammation. Turmeric, black pepper, undenatured type II collagen and frankincense resin are some stand out ingredients.

Illuminize - It helps to protect our eyes from damaging blue light found in our computers, mobile devices and the sun. It helps to increase macular pigment optical density (MPOD),which means it helps lower the risk of age related macular degeneration. It is a natural combination of acerola cherry, marigold flower and goji berry which supports eye and skin health.

Whole psyllium husk - Brushes out my colon and keeps it all moving through!

Young Living Super C Chewables - I like chewables, super easy and yummy.

Young Living Super Vitamin D Chewables - Support the immune and respiratory systems with 250 percent of the daily value of vitamin D. Vitamin D plays a key function in respiratory health through innate and adaptive defense mechanisms. Super Vitamin D also supports bone growth and healthy muscles. It's made with lemon balm extract and lime and melissa premium essential oils, which support mood and hormone regulation.

How I put it all together in the morning:
First I drink 24 oz of warm\hot water with lemon.

Then I make a 12 oz warm\hot water with a scoop of ICP Daily, Sulfurzyme and Aminowise.

Next I have 12 oz warm\hot water with 2oz Ningxia Red, a tbsp of psyllium husk, a few drops of tangerine and nutmeg oil and a squirt of Sunnectar Stevia.

OTHER FOUNDATIONAL PRODUCTS I USE EVERY DAY

Detoxzyme or Essentialzymes - A myriad of enzymes that complete digestion, help detoxify and promote cleansing. I take one an hour before my main meal. Live enzymes are where it's at! They are little magical catalysts that do so much of the work in your body. They facilitate breaking food down, making vitamins bioavailable, assisting chemical reactions and building tissue up. Ya. All of that! They are mysterious in that they get recycled and return to their original state after they do their work. Without enzymes our bodies' chemical reactions would be so slow that we wouldn't survive. When you look at food on a shelf at the grocery store it doesn't matter what the nutritional label says, if it is shelf stable it's dead and has no live enzymes, good for the company who sells it. Not good for you. I take digestive enzymes with every meal. It is a super easy thing you can do to improve your overall health. We also take them on the cleanse because when your body is not digesting solid food, it uses the enzymes to break down yukky stuff!

Life 9 Probiotic - Probiotics are live organisms that make up the good bacteria in your gut. They make a nice environment for your digestion. Life 9 includes 9 probiotic strains for full-spectrum gut support.

Sunrider Fortune Delight Tea - Detoxifying with anti-aging antioxidants. This delicious super tea targets cleaning the fat cells!

Sunrider Sunectar or Sunnydew - An antioxidant-rich stevia formula that helps regulate blood sugar. Chrysanthemum adds essential minerals like calcium, magnesium, folate, potassium.

JUST ADD HOT WATER

Water is the strongest solvent on earth, capable of dissolving more substances than any other liquid. Our body needs water to perform basically every essential function. "Drink more water." How many times have we heard this? Yet if something doesn't give me a hit, I am not going to do it. Cold water, from even the purest wells or springs never gave me a hit. It took me a long time to figure out how I was going to incorporate drinking more water into my routine. Let's face it, it is much more fun to eat than drink. I don't like drinking out of the tap or drinking out of plastic bottles or ice water at restaurants. A room temperature water out of a glass? Eh. I would get very thirsty and hold my breath and gulp some water down and that was about it. The master cleanse helped me awaken to the benefits I experienced on a liquid diet. I noticed the deficiency of water in daily life when I would come off a cleanse. I decided to develop a routine of drinking water when I actually felt the difference, the lack, in my mind and body. My cells were calling for water. One of my yoga teachers recommended hot water. She always had a thermos of hot water next to her in class and I thought, Oh I might like that. Guess what? I did.

The Chinese have a custom of drinking hot water and it goes way beyond simple preference. Hot water is considered a cure all. According to traditional Chinese medicine, the human body is made up of *yin* and *yang* elements. Good health is a balance of Yin *(negative, dark, feminine)* and Yang (positive, bright, masculine). If the *yang* gets too strong, which is easy to happen in our Yang based world, the body's internal temperature rises, and that person becomes susceptible to more illnesses. A simple way to get rid of the extra *Yang*, or excess heat, is by consuming food and drinks in the *Yin* category. Hot water is a *Yin* beverage. It is believed to lower the body's internal temperature, restoring balance and health. It is also believed to promote blood circulation, detoxify the body and relax the muscles. Cold water is said to have the opposite effect, slowing organ function and causing muscle contractions. Hot water also breaks up mucus in the body. It aids digestion, helps soften waste in the colon, it can improve central nervous system function and decrease stress levels.

I love carrying my hot water thermos with me! It is like a hot water bottle, it comforts me. I put a splash of lime oil in mine, you could use lemon or tangerine. Young Living makes a Vitality line of delicious and emotionally beneficial oils you can add.

TIP: Find a thermos you like the shape of in your hands, one you really like the way your mouth feels around the opening. This is important. I like Iron Flask, 17oz. I don't prefer to drink hot water out of a mug or a glass, it doesn't stay hot enough for me. I don't enjoy a huge 32 oz thermos, too much pressure to drink it all. Experiment for yourself with different vessels. You can even write loving words on your vessel! Water responds to positive thoughts and emotions!

I usually finish drinking my whole thermos before I grab a snack. That way I can better determine if this is appetite or is it thirst I am feeling. Most of the time I am refreshed with hot water.

I like to make hot water in a glass kettle. It doubles as a water feature in my environment. Bubbling moving water I can see, it's good feng shui!

Drink pure water. The best is right out of a mountain spring. Google springs near you, you may find one! The next best option is an alkalizing water purifying machine that makes ionized alkaline water such as Kangen or Tyent, or at least a Berkey water filter.

Do not drink *flavored* water. All *flavors* are basically the same, natural or artificial, they are not food. They are chemicals.

STINK

When I was in Junior High, a girl came in wearing a head wrap and she was pissed. She said she mixed two shampoos and there was an explosion on her head that burned her scalp. I always remembered this. Two shampoos could cause a reaction like this? Really? Isn't shampoo, soap? WTF? I did think shampoos smelled really fake and I was skeptical of them. I just started scrubbing my scalp and rinsing my head with only water. I thought soap dispensers in public restrooms and fancy liquid soaps in people's homes gave me a headache and the chemical scents stayed on my hands forever.

As I got older, I didn't understand shaving my armpits, making micro cuts under my arms in such a sensitive spot and then applying smelly stuff on top. And what's with all the breast cancer? hmmmmmm. I bought my personal and household products at the health food store but I still thought a lot of things smelled like chemicals. I saw how most products were about packaging and advertising. I wasn't a big label reader, my nose told me everything I needed to know and was instantly turned off by most products.

There is a documentary the chemical industry

doesn't want you to see.

It is called STINK. Fragrance doesn't come from a flower field in France, it comes from a chemical plant in New Jersey. Watch it on YouTube.

In the US, the regulations on personal care and household products are barely enforced and not regulated by the FDA. Corporations are not responsible for substantiating the safety of the ingredients in their products before we buy them. The European Union has banned over 1300 ingredients from cosmetic products. The US has banned 11.

CAVEAT EMPTOR. Let the buyer beware...Sure! We can all become chemists so we can read ingredient labels to make informed choices!

GREENWASHING: The process of conveying a false impression or providing misleading information about how a company's products are environmentally friendly. It is a play on the term *White Washing*, which means *using misleading information to gloss over bad behavior.*

Many companies practice Greenwashing by using terms such as *natural, organic, plant based.* They mean *nothing.* It is extremely manipulative as these corporations know that we, the consumers, want healthier products but instead of making healthier products, they say whatever they want on the label to trick us into buying what we think is a healthier product.

Using words such as organic, natural, lavender, is cheaper than sourcing plants, adhering to safer farming practices and using quality ingredients. Not only is this profit driven, it is diabolically profit driven. Take a multinational corporation, Johnson & Johnson. They develop personal care products as well as pharmaceuticals and medical devices. People use their pharmaceutical drugs and medical devices when we develop allergies, eczema, respiratory problems and cancer from the chemicals in their personal care products. Look up Johnson's Baby Powder and cancer.

Avoid some of the biggest culprits. Four of them are endocrine disruptors.

ENDOCRINE DISRUPTORS are chemicals found in many personal care and household products. They interfere with the synthesis, secretion, transport, binding, action, or elimination of natural hormones in the body that are responsible for development, behavior, fertility, and maintenance of homeostasis (normal cell metabolism). These disruptions can cause cancerous tumors, birth defects, and other developmental disorders such as learning disabilities, attention deficit disorder, cognitive and brain development problems.

1. PARABENS - A cheap preservative that allows corporations to protect their profits by extending a product's shelf life found in makeup, moisturizers, hair care and shaving products. A study in the Journal of Applied Toxicology found there can be large quantities of parabens in breast cancer tumors. They may mimic natural estrogen in the body. They bind to estrogen receptors and encourage malfunction in the body for both women and men as well as being linked to the

onset of early puberty and sterility in men.

2. PHTHALATES - A group of chemicals used to make plastics more flexible. They are in children's toys, food packaging, shampoos, detergents, etc. They are tiny plastic molecules in fragrances to keep the scent lingering in the air. When you smell cologne or perfume you are inhaling plastic. UGH. Phthalates are linked to breast cancer, developmental issues, decreased fertility, obesity and asthma.

3. MINERAL OIL and PARAFFIN WAX - mineral oil is not made from stones or crystals...It is a petroleum (crude oil) by-product used in baby oils, chapstick, vaseline, candles and more.

4. FRAGRANCE - This is a BIG ONE. Fragrance is a catch phrase corporations use to hide a cocktail of potentially hundreds of chemicals under the guise of "trade secrets". Fragrance is used in cosmetics, toiletries, household products, laundry soap, air fresheners, candles, etc.

And then there is....

5. SODIUM LAURYL SULPHATE (SLS) - A cheap foaming agent derived from a petroleum byproduct. Hmmm... another way to make money from crude oil. Put it in beauty products! Yuk. SLS interferes with the skin's natural ability to regulate and protect itself. But if it foams it means it's getting you cleaner, right? No. SLS is a known skin irritant. It's commonly used in lab testing to intentionally irritate animal skin. (Think beagles

and rabbits). They irritate the animal's skin to test the efficacy of products intended to heal skin. Super creepy. SLS causes problems such as skin and eye irritations, dermatitis, eczema, psoriasis, hormonal disruptions, dizziness and headaches.

It is difficult to control the chemicals in our environment, but we can be the guardians at the gate of our homes! We vote with our dollars and decide what to buy, what comes inside. It doesn't have to be that complicated. Start by not purchasing products with these ingredients and these nasties will not be clogging, confusing and poisoning our bodies.

I keep it simple and order all my household and personal care products from Young Living Essential Oils. They are a beautiful gift the plants give to us. They are cultivated from roots, rinds, leaves, bark, seeds and flowers and distilled from the most powerful part of the plant, the lifeblood, the part of the plant that enacts change. Think about the difference between a leaf on a tree or one on the ground that has dried up that has lost its lifeblood. Moving and shaking, just like our blood clots our cuts, oxygenates our cells and detoxifies our bodies, oils work through trauma and energize the plant. They do the same thing for us when they are unadulterated and pure.

Young Living is the modern day innovator of essential oils. They started as a mom and pop shop that has grown in thirty years, to set the global standard for the highest quality of essential oils on earth. Young Living's Seed to Seal Certification are exacting methods of cultivation, distillation and testing, you can check out the website seedtoseal.com for more information. Introducing the plant kingdom through Young Living products has opened passages of communication in my body, upgraded my health and my intuition so much so I can't help but share how much I love them. Then I started getting paid to turn my friends on to the products creating passive income. Passive income is not just for movie stars and rock gods! Although we are not taught about it in school, it is money you work for once yet you keep getting paid on.

Before I experienced Young Living oils, I was exposed to essential oils at the health food store and I quickly passed them by as I could sense they were not the highest quality. Now I know what it takes to grow and cultivate and distill pure frankincense. Just remember this, if you see a big bottle of frankincense for 20 bucks, you know it's adulterated and will not give you true benefit. Many companies have jumped on the essential oil revolution for profit only. They are concerned only with yield and fragrance. They are not interested in the chemical constituents in essential oils that can change DNA expressions. These chemical constituents are classified into three compounds, phenylpropanoids, which clean receptor sites, sesquiterpenes, which go into DNA and delete negative inherited programing and monoterpenes, which reprogram the DNA blueprint for positive change.

Three ways to use Young Living essential oils:

1. Topically : Apply to your wrists, neck, brain stem, lower back and on the bottom of your feet.

2. Aromatically : This is a very effective way to use

oils. Our nose hairs are great receptors for oils. From there, it's a short path to our olfactory bulbs and then the limbic region of our brain, playing a role in our emotions, memories and behavior. These are things we want to have a handle on!

3. Internally : The Vitally Line is designed to use internally. Add drops in your water, add to your recipes or just drop oil under your tongue.

Note: I would not ingest other brands of essential oils. I know the quality of Young Living.

Essential oils are absorbed into your bloodstream and metabolized, so even when you can't smell them anymore, they have benefits on the body, mind and spirit. Whereas, fragrance and synthetics clog, limit and confuse our bodies.

EIGHT LIMBS

"Replace the question, What will Yoga do for me? with How may I serve thee, Lord? Let love be your guide. When you love what you do, the means to do it will be revealed to you."

–Sharon Gannon and David Life

Yoga means union. It comes from the Sanskrit root yuj, to unite, to yoke the separate self with the universal Self. It is the perfect practice for slipping into to 5D!

In *Patanjali's Yoga Sutra*, the eightfold path presented is called ashtanga, which means eight limbs in Sanskrit. These are guidelines on how to live. They teach us how to take care of ourselves, morally, ethically and how to care for our health and spirit through self discipline.

1. YAMAS - external disciplines
Ahimsa - non violence
Satya - truthfulness
Asteya - non stealing
Brahmacharya - right use of energy

Aparigraha - non hoarding

2. NIYAMAS - internal disciplines
Saucha - cleanliness
Santosha - contentment
Tapas - discipline or burning desire
Svadhyaya - self study
Isvara Pranidhana - surrender to a higher power

3. ASANA - posture
4. PRANAYAMA - breathwork
5. PRATYAHARA - sense withdrawal
6. DHARANA - focused concentration
7. DHYANA - meditation
8. SAMADHI - enlightenment

BREATH IS BOSS

"The breath knows how to go deeper than the mind."

–Wim Hof

Our mind is developed as an instrument of fear. That's a good thing. It is wired to keep us safe. You have done a fabulous job, mind! You can stand down now, you can stop patrolling the borders and let other gifts we have come front and center. We're good, thank you. We are no longer fighting for our survival every moment of every day.

We can do more fun things like we can engage our clairs in a treasure hunt, we can relax, we can enjoy grace and ease, we can create. There are many things we can do other than spend our days constantly following our overworked minds, constructing ways to keep us safe.

If you look around, you can see many people following their minds all day long, living in constant survival mode. It's very common and it's very 3D. It's fine, no need to rush them, that is where they need to be, running around, using their heads instead of their breath. It is not surprising though because in our culture scholars get scholarships and yogis get the old side eye. There are no prizes for self control of our thoughts. Even though gaining control over your thoughts allows you to have much better control over your emotions. Thoughts trigger your emotions and once your emotions are involved, they can take over fast and run wild. They are much harder to turn around once they get involved.

We are not our thoughts. We have thoughts but we are not our thoughts and the thoughts we have may not even be our own as we have been discussing. They could be coming from many places, the collective consciousness (other radio stations), subliminal messages inserted in the media or your subconscious programming. They can be your parents' thoughts. You know when you sound just like them?

It doesn't matter where they came from. When you use this meditation regularly, you become good at identifying and releasing thoughts in your day. When you recognize a negative thought, or even speak a negative thought, you catch it. You can just say, "Hey that is not mine! Cancel cancel delete delete, on with the Treasure Hunt!"

When we allow a thought to pass through our mind, not stringing it together with other thoughts, not making deductions or judgements, we can let them go. We become open to what lies beyond. The world is not happening to you. Your life is 100% a reflection of your thoughts. Your thoughts create your environment, your health, bank account and your relationships.

Focusing on your breath helps you get hold of your thoughts. There is a reason the first thing we do when we come into this body is breathe and it's the last thing we do when we leave. We don't think, we breathe. When you have control of your thoughts, when you are riding on top of them, you decide how you perceive and respond to 3D reality. You decide what comes into focus. You decide what to create.

READY. SET. FIVE MINUTES A DAY.

Put ten drops each of Frankincense and Orange in your diffuser.
Apply *YL Deep Relief Roll On* to the back of your neck.
Sit up straight.
Relax your shoulders.
Set a timer for five minutes.
Close your eyes and concentrate on your inhalation and exhalation.
Take a four count inhalation.
Inhale. Inhale. Inhale. Inhale.
Take a four count exhalation.
Exhale. Exhale. Exhale. Exhale.
As a thought arises, recognize it.
Oh that's a thought.
Let it go.
Return to counting.
Inhale. Inhale. Inhale. Inhale.
When another thought arises, do the same thing, notice

it and let it pass.

That's a thought. That's not me.

Return to your inhalation and exhalation.

If you find yourself stringing thoughts together, getting all caught up in the conversation, deducting, blaming, making lists, it is OK. You can become aware of the stream of thoughts at any time, catch them trying to be boss and put them in their place.

Return to counting your breath.
Inhale. Inhale. Inhale. Inhale.
Exhale. Exhale. Exhale. Exhale.

At first there will be a constant stream of thoughts. Eventually they will slow and you will have space between them. This is when Breath is Boss. Practice everyday, working up to 30 minutes. You will get better and better and go longer and longer defying time as a construct. You will have new perceptions, clarity and confidence in your 5D time!

Another way to look at meditation of all kinds is that meditation puts you in the receiving mode, like a radio, receiving a broadcast. If you are having trouble with meditation, tune the dial on your radio receiver first. Let your team know that you are getting ready to receive guidance from them by using techniques such as mantra recitation, drumming, yoga asana, whatever works to get you in the receiving mode.

TIME IS A MANMADE CONSTRUCT

"Time seems to be the dimension about which we have the greatest anxiety. Perhaps because it's the dimension in which we see with the least clarity. Numerous peoples have dealt with this lack of clarity by developing various methods of divination."

–Terence McKenna

The contemporary conception of time was created for the purpose of paying wages during the industrial revolution. It has been so strictly and uniformly drilled into us that we have forgotten that it was developed for reasons of control. Our clocks are a hodgepodge of cultures, a little Egyptian, a little Babylonian, a little French. To avoid accidents in the US, standardized time zones were put in place with the advent of railroads crossing quickly through large expanses of local time zones. Eventually all countries were forced to adhere to the Greenwich Mean Time for world wide trading purposes. Britain alone had many different local times. Members of Parliament pushed for a standard so they knew exactly how long they had to get their drink on in the pubs. Yes, standardization of time is related to alcohol.

Common sayings about time that limit our imagination and creative play:

I don't have time to do this.
The clock is ticking.
We haven't got all day.
Time flies when we are having fun.
(Which really implies, time flies when we are not exchanging time for money.)

TIP: Early birds have more fun. Arrive early to the man made construct of time. When you give a nod to the construct by arriving earlier than the clock told you to, you beat the system. Not just arriving on time, on time people can easily become late. Arriving early gives you more free time when you get somewhere! You can access the situation, get your pick of seats, people watch, prepare, relax. You have used the fake system to your advantage. You also have time to deal with unexpected issues, traffic, etc., that cause stress to even *on time* people.

This is such an easier ride than people who rebel against this system and are *late people.* A late person unconsciously feels the falseness of the construct yet is only hurting themselves and others who have hustled and stressed themselves to be on time.

You are enough and you do enough. Start off by scheduling less things in your day. Leave hours and hours between appointments. Over estimate travel time. Become an early person to have more joy and relaxation when you do need to follow the 3D construct.

MAKING THE MOST OF
OUR SUBCONSCIOUS

"The great secret possessed by the great men of all ages was their ability to contact and release the powers of their subconscious mind. You can do the same."

– Joseph Murphy

The conscious mind makes up a very small percentage of our brain activity. It's our analytical, creative mind, the part of our brain that learns from books, tutorials, from everyday experiences. Let's say the conscious mind is the captain of a big ship.

The subconscious mind makes up most of our brain activity. It is a large database of our beliefs, our skills, our memories. It also regulates the automatic part of our nervous system, blood flow, heartbeat and digestive processes, basically the functions that keep us safe and alive.

Our subconscious mind is programmed in the first seven years of our lives. Children, little tape recorders, areliving in the hypnotic theta brain wave state. They are constantly taking in behavior they see all around them so when consciousness kicks in, they have programs to work with, they know what to expect and how to navigate life. Let's say the subconscious mind is like the whole ship and all of the crew put together.

The captain (conscious mind) plans the route, steers the ship and gives the orders. The crew (subconscious mind) carries out the orders, automatically, no questions asked, a very efficient system! Yet if the crew is not getting new updated orders from the captain because the conscious mind doesn't know how to communicate properly with the subconscious mind or it is overridden by a psychoactive, mind altering drug like caffeine, it is not a very efficient system!

The captain tries harder to communicate, it brings out its most powerful tool, *Willpower.* Well, even using brute force, we all know willpower only works for a short time. As soon as the conscious mind gets exhausted, the subconscious mind will take over and start playing those golden oldie tapes with patterns and habits just trying to keep you alive, not to help you thrive and live your fullest richest life. We can look at our lives with our conscious mind and see clearly what our subconscious programming is. Whatever is working is good programming you received from your parents and your community up to age seven. Whatever is not working in your life, whatever seems stuck, whatever gives you trouble over and over again, financial problems, relationship problems, health issues, are all just negative programming you received. You don't have to go to therapy and figure out the causes of your problems, you can simply give your subconscious new working orders!

Use *your twilight state to your advantage!* There is a special time when your subconscious mind is easy to influence. It is the thin veil between the waking and the sleeping state. We enter this relaxed, hypnotic state, the theta brain wave state, when we drift off to sleep and when we arise from deep sleep. During this time, your subconscious mind is open for instructions. Be mindful of what you are thinking about and use this nodding off and awakening time wisely with intention! This is not the time to think of the past or go over hurtful things. It is the time to imagine your incredible dream life in detail and how this new life actually makes you feel! Get in there! Get juicy! Look forward and feel the feelings of your desires already manifested in your life at this special time! Your thoughts and emotions have powerful frequency!

FREQUENCY IS EVERYTHING

"If you want to find the secrets of the Universe, think in terms of energy, frequency and vibration."

–Nikola Tesla

The systems in our body are made up of tissues and organs, which are made up of cells. Billions of cells are made up of molecules, molecules are made up of atoms, which are made up of subatomic particles. When you put subatomic particles under a microscope they are made up of 99.999% space. This is where there is a field of information that can be read as frequency! It is the Akashic records, the quantum field. The quality of this field and the access we have to it, determines the physical, emotional and the mental experience we are having in these bodies.

I use an amazing little device called Healy to communicate directly to that space! Healy analyzes specific frequencies in the body that are causing imbalances and delivers specific frequencies to bring the body back into bioenergetic balance. The frequencies the device delivers impact our DNA, helping it to unwind and express itself more fully!

The quantum sensor in it sees you in your highest expression and scans and delivers a new custom frequency just for you every ten seconds. It gathers information and chooses programs for you to unblock and move energy in your body, creating coherence between your heart, body and head. We are not just mechanics and chemicals, we are electromagnetic beings with electric thoughts and magnetic feelings!

Healy also has technology that offers an easy way to change our subconscious programming! It addresses the epigenetic component of our cells. The quantum sensor finds our subconscious triggers and chips away at our subconscious programming, heads it off at the pass, before it can lead to problems! Using the quantum field to amplify our prophecies and intentions as well as backing them up with our emotions is super powerful! Healy doesn't do the work, we do. Feeling the feelings of your desires already manifested in your life, is the crucial work that only you can do when you are ready.

Tip: We are cosmic conscious creators and when we experience the feelings of our desires already manifested in our lives, it takes us from a state of wishing and wanting into a place of it just being so.

Incorporating these frequencies into my daily routines and habits have put me on the expressway!

I have let go of deep rooted patterns in my life as well as helped clients do the same. Healy is pushing easy buttons for big transformation!

DAYS OF GRATITUDE

Gratitude puts you in an emotionally receiving mode. Every morning for a month make a list of ten things you are grateful for. They can be as simple as your next breath, your family, your toenail polish, just get ten things you are grateful for on a piece of paper as quickly as you can. Don't think, just write. This is also a really good way to get your writing juices flowing. You can do this by yourself or you get a few friends and do a challenge for a month. Anytime I am feeling lacking I make a gratitude list!

Example:

Day 1

1. I am grateful for this breath.
2. I am grateful for this pen and paper.
3. I am grateful for my friends.
4. I am grateful for my body that carries me around all day.
5. I am grateful for the clothes on my body.
6. I am grateful for the morning light coming in the

window that's warming me.

7. I am grateful for the birds singing in the trees. Oh, they are actually telling me to feed them.
8. I am so grateful to be able to understand their needs!
9. I am so grateful I have birdseed!
10. I am so grateful to be able to go outside and feed them.

At first your gratitude is a little stiff and seems silly but once you get rolling, get flowing, it can be astounding and feel so good. Crack open the transformative, magical practice of gratitude. Just get started!

NIGHTLIFE

"I have a dream."

–Martin Luther King, Jr.

"A real dreamer is always hunting his power. He goes out every night like a hunter with a net, to stalk his dreams. The more dreams he catches the more powerful he becomes."

–Shonnounkouiretsi, Mohawk Shaman

"A dream uninterpreted is a letter unopened."

–Unknown

"Write your dreams."

–Jim Morrison to Nico, on songwriting

There is a great movement afoot to rebirth a dreaming society and re-enchant the world. Join us! Do you remember your dreams? Dreams are another reality, full of messages, guides, clues, even prophecies. If you do not honor your dreams you are missing out on a richer, more exciting life, full of travel and intrigue. Imagine all of the places you can go, the people you can spend time with both alive and those who have passed on. All you have to do is close your eyes. That is why I love dream travel, it's so practical and simple. You are going to go to sleep anyway, why not take advantage of this time for experiences and insights? It's more time spent out of the construct! You may even wake up in your dreams, lucid dreaming.

START A DREAM JOURNAL

Writing down your dreams is how you catch them. This is an art form, a practice, another way to slip into 5D from 3D. The more you do it, the more dreams you will remember. Write down everything even if it is just a wisp or a feeling. My dream journal is a place I go for information. I can review dreams and see different messages from old friends, relatives or guides who have visited with things to tell me. I am reminded to look for them in my waking life.

Before you fall asleep, state out loud "I remember my dreams!" Diffuse Young Living Dream Catcher essential oil at bedtime. Write out a question or ask for help and place it under your pillow with a mugwort leaf and lavender pillow. When I do this, the answer comes in a day or two!

HONOR YOUR DREAMS

Write down the entire dream, every detail you remember as soon as you wake up.
Give each dream a title.
Write down the theme of the dream.
Write down the emotions you remember from this dream.

Make a sketch or a painting from your dream.

Could this dream happen in waking life?

Did this dream possibly happen in waking life?

Did you spot any spirit guides in it?

What music did you hear in your dream? Record it on a voice memo.

Carry your dream into waking life with a memento. Pick out an object from your dream and display it or wear a color from your dream.

Start a symbol dictionary of recurring symbols from your dreams.

Start a *Dream Power* Group with your friends to discuss your dreams.

FALL FLAT ON YOUR FAITH

"Nature rewards courage."

–Terence McKenna

"Die before you die."

–Sufi saying

There is a magic, hidden, powerful path that only reveals itself when you fall flat on your faith. Maybe something pivotal has happened, something that you were not expecting, but here it is. You can no longer do the things you have always done to get the results you have always gotten. Suddenly staying small and safe becomes more painful or impossible, than taking a blind step forward. You know that you may trip, fall, scrape your hands and knees and get the wind knocked out of you. You have no plan, no map or trail, only faith that everything is working out for you. You follow your clairs and you boldly step forward in the dark.

Now here is where the magic comes in. Shuffling along at first, getting caught up in weeds, this is exactly how you allow your path to become clear. There is a faint illumination, enough to see one foot in front of you at a time. You keep going. Finally you look up and you can see your way! Now there are others with you! Where is this light coming from? Oh, the illumination is coming from inside you.

To be continued...

APPENDIX

RECOMMENDED READING:

The Hidden Messages In Water
Masuru Emoto

We'Moon
Gaia Rhythms for Womyn

Essential Oils Desk Reference
Life Science Publishing

Supplements Desk Reference
2nd Edition
Jen O'Sullivan

Non Violent Communication
Marshall B Rosenberg

The Complete Master Cleanse
Tom Woloshyn

Healing In The Age of Enlightenment
Stanley Burroughs

Heal Your Body
Louise Hay

Jivamukti Yoga
Sharon Gannon and David Life

My Word Made Flesh
Awakening Your Health And Wealth Through The Words you Speak (first edition if you can get it)
Robert Tennyson Stevens and Marcella Von Harding, PhD

Alcohol Explained
Williaim Potter

Species Of Amnesia
Robert Sepehr

RECOMMENDED DOCUMENTARIES:

Cult of The Medics

The Promise on Bitchute.com (The history of mammograms and their accuracy)

STINK on Youtube.com

RECOMMENDED PRODUCTS:

Here is my email: rcd.rae@gmail.com

Let me know if you have any questions, I would love to chat with you!

Young Living Essential Oils
My Referral # 16370256 and email me for a discount code.

Sunrider International
Email me for a discount code.

Healy Personal Frequency Device
Email me for a discount code.

Vitaliseur de Marion Soft Steamer.
Email me for a discount code

ABOUT THE AUTHOR

Rae Leonard

Rae is a recovering native New Yorker turned Intuitive Artist and Transformationalist. She guides her coterie with relish, giving sparkling energetic adjustments charged with love, relief and comfort. You might spot her somewhere along the Eastern Seaboard in her Sprinter. She could possibly be deciphering notes from napkins outside Stone Age Kitchen in Chestertown or nodding off in a hammock in the Hudson Valley. Very often she's near the fountain at Forsyth Park in Savannah, waiting for the owls to land and quench their thirst at dusk.

www.ingramcontent.com/pod-product-compliance
Lightning Source LLC
Chambersburg PA
CBHW072349090426
42741CB00012B/2987